MR. **M**OJO RISIN'

Jim Morrison
The Last Holy Fool

As Magic Jim begins his sermon on the mount two more disciples rise up to catch the hallucinated loaves and fishes. Magic Mountain outdoor concert, Marin County, Calif., 1967. (Photograph by Gene Anthony)

RIGHT

The beautiful monster lurching in the wake of the Doors' soft machine. Magic Mountain outdoor concert, Marin County, Calif., 1967. (Photograph by Gene Anthony)

The Alien beginning to break out of the *puto*. Winterland, San Francisco, Calif., December, 1967. (Photograph by Baron Wolman)

MR. MOJO RISIN'

Jim Morrison

The LAST HOLY FOOL

by David Dalton

Foreword by Nick Tosches

ST. Martin's Press

PRODUCED AND DESIGNED BY Spade & Archer, Inc.

Mr. Mojo Risin'

Jim Morrison
The Last Holy Fool

Grateful acknowledgment is made to the following
authors and publishers for permission to reprint from:
"Grahr Mantra" from *Star* by Michael McClure, pub-
lished by Grove Press © 1964, 1965, 1966, 1968,
1970 by Michael McClure/ "Riddym Ravings" by
Jean "Binta" Breeze in *Voiceprint,* edited by Stewart
Brown, Mervyn Morris and Gordon Rohler, pub-
lished by Longman Group UK Limited © Longman
Group UK Limited 1989/"Song of Encouragement,"
from *Singing for Power* by Ruth Murray Underhill ©
1938 by the Regents of the University of California,
University of California Press/"The Lizard," from
The Collected Poems of D.H. Lawrence, by D.H.
Lawrence, edited by Vivian de Sola Pinto and F.
Warren Roberts. Copyright © 1964, 1971, by
Angelo Ravagli and C. Mary Weekley, executors of
the estate of Frieda Lawrence Ravagli. Reprinted by
permission of Viking Penguin a division of Penguin
Books USA Inc.

Grateful acknowledgment is made to Doors Music
Company for permission to quote from the follow-
ing songs:
"The Changeling," Lyrics by Jim Morrison, Music
by The Doors © 1971 Doors Music Co. "Peace
Frog," Lyrics by Jim Morrison, Music by The Doors
© 1970 Doors Music Co. "Moonlight Drive,"
Words and Music by The Doors © 1967 Doors
Music Co. "Break on Through," Words and Music
by The Doors © 1966 Doors Music Co. "Love
Street," Words and Music by The Doors © 1968
Doors Music Co. "The Crystal Ship," Words and
Music by The Doors © 1967 Doors Music Co.
"Strange Days," Words and Music by The Doors ©
1967 Doors Music Co. "When the Music's Over,"
Words and Music by The Doors © 1967 Doors
Music Co. "Five to One," Words and music by The
Doors © 1968 by Doors Music Co. "Roadhouse
Blues," Lyrics by Jim Morrison, Music by The
Doors © 1970 Doors Music Co. "Maggie M'Gill,"
Lyrics by Jim Morrison, Music by The Doors ©
1970 Doors Music Co. "Shaman's Blues," Words
and Music by Jim Morrison © 1969 Doors Music
Co. "Horse Latitudes," Words and Music by The
Doors © 1968 Doors Music Co.

Library of Congress Cataloging-in-Publication Data
Dalton, David.
   Mr. Mojo Risin': Jim Morrison, The
Last Holy Fool/text by David Dalton.
    ISBN 0-312-05900-0 (hardcover)—
    ISBN 0-312-05899-3 (pbk).
    1. Morrison, Jim, 1943-1971. 2. Rock
musicians—United States—Biography.
I. Title. II. Title: Mister Mojo Risin'.
ML420.M62D3 1991
782.42166'092—dc20
[B]

                    90-28608
                      CIP

First Edition: April 1991

10 9 8 7 6 5 4 3 2 1

Angelino bands were generally suspect at the Avalon Ballroom, the sanctum sanctorum of Haight-geist, but when the Doors hit them with their psychocinematic *Anschluss,* "The End," what could they say but "Far-fuckin' out, man!" San Francisco, Calif., 1967. (Photograph © 1967 Bobby Klein, courtesy FAHEY/KLEIN Gallery, Los Angeles)

Jim: "I read in the paper that some headshrink says people like me who perform on stage are crazy....I read that they didn't get enough love when they were kids....I didn't get enough love." "He's got a hard on," the chick behind me whispered. It looked as if she was right. Hollywood Bowl, Hollywood, Calif., 1970. (Photograph by Ed Caraeff)

ontents

"**how
your meat, Jim, never
known it to fail."
Famous Morrison post-
masturbation shot,
Venice Beach, Calif.,
1967. (Photograph
© 1967 Bobby Klein,
courtesy FAHEY/KLEIN
Gallery, Los Angeles)**

Foreword

James Douglas **M**orrison

1943–1971

Jersey City, June 1968 "Hello, I Love You." I remember not only where I was but also whom I was with when it came through the balmy early-summer air like the resurrection gust of Enyalios.

That's right: Enyalios. I knew the Doors, but I didn't then know of Enyalios. He was, I later found out, an ancient, forgotten god of destruction, a god whose name had lain hidden on clay tablets in Knossos from the second millennium B.C. until the turn of this century. The name had gone unuttered until the decipherment by Michael Ventris—just fifteen or so years before that summer of 1968—of the hermetic script, Mycenaean Linear B, that harbored it. Soon, just a few months after "Hello, I Love You," the publication of Charles Olson's *Maximus Poems IV, V, VI* would evoke the god as Enyalion, summoning the full force of the word power that seemed to tie the archaic Greek *Enyalios* of Linear B with the classical Greek *anileon* ("merciless"), the Latin *ad nihil* ("to" + "nothing") and *annihilare* ("to render unto nothingness"), and our own *annihilate*.

As I said, I didn't know any of this back then; and I didn't care, either. All I was concerned with on that June day—there were three of us—was ditching the guy and making the girl. I got lucky. But I really don't remember that part. What I remember is that gust of annihilation that in two minutes and fourteen seconds destroyed and delivered us from the utter bullshit that had been the sixties. We were free again, those of us who did not stink of patchouli, believe in the family of man, or eat macrobiotic gruel; those of us who found god—he dressed well—through smack, preferred our sex dirty, and supported our boys in Vietnam because it meant a surplus of left-behind pussy on the home front.

Of course, Morrison and the Doors had been instrumental to what was now being annihilated. The summer of 1967, the Summer of Love—was it *Time* magazine's phrase, was it Timothy Leary's, was there any difference, really?—had also been the summer of "Light My Fire." Jim Morrison became to rock 'n' roll the embodiment of every romantic pretension, from Rimbaud to shamanism, that its consumers, in those days of innocence, held so dear. It soon became apparent, however, that Jim Morrison, his figure ever darker and more estranged, wasn't only writing and singing rock 'n' roll songs but was also trying to vanquish his demons and curses by invoking new demons and curses. "I am the Lizard King. I can do anything," he had the strange, young nerve to say and believe.

"Light My Fire," the beckoning, the seduction, and "Hello, I Love You," the banishing—the only Doors songs to become number-one hits—were separated by a year. It happened that fast. The romanticism of "Light My Fire" had enthralled, but the death's-head within that flaming, Augustinian heart, that equation of love and the funeral pyre, went unheeded. Its singer was likened to Apollo and, as his excesses became legendary, to Dionysus—when in fact more fitting, albeit equally callow, comparison might have been made, if not to obscure Enyalios himself, then to Apollyon, the Destroyer, the angel of the bottomless pit, "that old serpent" of Revelation 20:1. ("Ride the snake. He's old, and his skin is cold." Morrison, in "The End," would give those words the air of an elusive ancestral memory emerging from blackness to consciousness.)

"The Beatles' spiritual teacher speaks to the youth of the world on love and the untapped source of power that lies within," hawked the full-page advertisement in *Billboard* for the album by Maharishi Mahesh Yogi. That was in April 1968. The whole vast noisome toilet bowl of love, peace, and direct-marketing ahimsa was overflowing all over the fucking place. So, it was love they wanted. Love was all they needed. Well, that summer, Morrison delivered it, nasty and impersonal—"Hello, I love you, won't you tell me your name?"—like a cold hard blue-veined cock right up under the tie-dyed skirts of benighted sensitivity.

Morrison and the Doors, significantly, were absent at that great New Age Rotarian convocation in the sticks known as Woodstock. His and the band's success had waned steadily since "Hello, I Love You." It was over, in a way. Morrison had put the spirit of the sixties out of its misery. But he seemed unable to put himself out of his own misery.

What he wanted more than anything—more than fame, more than wealth, more than the wet genital submission that those things brought—was to be taken seriously as a poet. But he was too full of lingering youth, too unfinished to sense how little he knew about the job of turning a vision into meaningful words and rhythms. The Doors' most ambitious work was often their worst. Trying to make of rock 'n' roll something it could never, should never be, Morrison often seemed a pompous fool rather than the intrepid seer he fancied himself. With dark messianic urgency, in both his songs and his verse, he delivered images and ideas that sometimes were trite unto embarrassment. In *An American Prayer,* the little volume of poetry he published in 1970, he asked, affectedly forsaking any question mark, "Do you know we are ruled by TV." We may be surprised by the banality of those words, or by their arrogance, but we aren't surprised by the fact that a vanity press published them.

But Morrison's boyish failings efface neither the sporadic, gestating beauty of his vision and talent nor the frustratingly immense promise of what might have been. He and the Doors, in their four, fast years in the world's eye, made a music unlike any other, and that music was more often brilliant than not. "Roadhouse Blues," with its wonderful kiss-off to all epistemology ("I woke up this morning and got myself a beer/The future's uncertain, the end is always near"), especially in the immediacy of the concert version recorded during the 1969-1970 *Absolutely Live* tour, remains by itself a solid enough plinth for rock 'n' roll immortality to rest upon.

Had Morrison lived, that immense promise likely might have been fulfilled, and he likely might have got what he wanted. But he died at the age of twenty-seven—the same age at which, in 1913, Ezra Pound (who had also been a vanity-press poet) declared: "Most important poetry has been written by men over thirty."

It's difficult not to view as entwined serpents the obsessions at the heart of Morrison's vision and the shortcut he took to the grave. Those obsessions—common to all, but in him overriding—were sex and death; and, while he wore the uraeus of those obsessions well and always, he looked upon them as impenetrable enemies lying within. The wedding-in-song of love and the funeral pyre could be perceived as a comely lyrical conceit in the summer of 1967. But by the end, libido and death wish were one, inseparable.

There were lines in the poem "An American Prayer" that overwhelmed its failings and illuminated its black-diamond glintings and the magnitude of its promise. But in that illumination lay a dire shadowing. As if betrothing himself to death, Morrison, annihilation's fair boy, sees her as "pale & wanton thrillful." Toward the poem's close, he says, with an almost Miltonic metrical precision: "Death makes angels of us all/& gives us wings." In "Lament for the Death of my Cock," recorded on his final birthday, December 8, 1970—it seemed more a day of mourning than of celebration—Morrison declares: "Death and my cock are the world." Ultimately, libido itself succumbs: "…I sacrifice my cock on the altar of silence." And silence came.

For once looking—backward maybe, it now might seem—toward life, Morrison says with quiet resolution in "Lament": "Words got me the wound and will get me well." But a few months later, he was dead, and that was that. America loves the self-killed, the notches in lurid tragedy's gun; and Jim Morrison in death has been raised to the realm of the mythic through media grave robbers and their patrons. What he might have become is something that we can never know. What we can be assured of is that the glimmerings and bursts of that possibility, that promise, are enough to grant his legacy a place outside the junkyard of unrenowned obscurity where most rock 'n' roll and poetry alike come justly in the end to decompose.

If only he could have conquered that Lady Death who "makes angels of us all," if only he had hurled her into the dirt the way he fucked the sixties into the dirt, maybe he would still be around. But, then again—enough fancy talk, enough shuck-and-jive—it's like the man says: Better him than us. Shoot the shaman and pass the pastafazool.

Nick Tosches

Prelude

Like others who died young and

under mysterious circumstances, Jim Morrison's life is read backward. His already larger-than-life reputation precipitated into a morbid and evangelical cult when he died under unexplained circumstances in a Paris hotel bathtub and his body was furtively buried without autopsy. Lives read through such a dark glass—Van Gogh, James Dean, Jimi Hendrix—lend themselves to fantastic fabrications and grotesque distortions.

Was he murdered? Did he OD from heroin? Cocaine? Speed? Alcohol? All four? Did his prematurely aged body just give out? Or was he the victim of a voodoo phone call from a jealous lover? Did he die elsewhere and was he then carried and placed in the bath to protect others? Or did he simply stage his own death, as he often threatened to do, and disappear into new life to write his epic?

Some may find all this hysterical and excessive, but Jim would have loved it. His heroes from an early age were Rimbaud, Dylan Thomas, romantic self-destructive geniuses, the Holy Fool, Van Gogh in flames, anarchic visionaries exhilarated by standing on the edge of the abyss and peering in.

And Morrison himself is the last in a long line of Pop messiahs, cowboy angels and beautiful, possessed, seraphic martyrs of youth and art. A direct descendant of James Dean, Jack Kerouac and Jackson Pollock.

"All alone... on a tightrope ride...." Winterland, San Francisco, Calif., December, 1967. (Photograph by Baron Wolman)

THE ORIGIN OF MOJO JIM

Jimi Hendrix, Janis Joplin, Jim Morrison...the psychotropic trinity. Avatars of the late sixties without whom the First Great Psychedelic Era could hardly be imagined. They were so perfect! Emblematic saints of excess and transcendence. Where did they come from? Did these precursors create their times or did the times merely create the conditions necessary for these contenders to thrive? "Such a man was wanted," said Ralph Waldo Emerson of this quandary, "and such a man was born."

Perhaps epochs preform out of the Great Unformed, molding the significant ones, deliverers, saints, criminals, rock stars, personal managers, the person who just asked you if anyone has called, million-records-in-sales certifiers, and this is the real meaning of It Is Written. It is encoded—how could it be otherwise?

Tiny, infinitesimal Janis Joplins, Jimi Hendrixes, Bob Dylans, immaculate homunculi and femunculi, twinklings of futurity, strung along the helical wires of DNA, millions of brightly colored molecules dancing and humming along the Neuron Highway. The unleavened ones (us!) already there, circa 1942–1945, latent in the great dough roll of history. The whole cast assembled, already out there!

James Douglas Morrison is born on December 8, 1943. And simultaneously on some dark asteroid in the utterness of howling space out pops Bad Jim, Krazy Jim, Grim Jim, Demon Jim, Mojo! Infinitely resourceful imp of the perverse, he is the crawling king snake, the terrible twin. Mr. Two-Time Baby. And out of this darkness comes "a monster, black dressed in leather," Mojo Jim from dimension X.

Do I discern the mark of the beast in the following passage from the memoir *Riders on the Storm*, by the Doors' drummer, John Densmore?

> After getting the song down on tape, Jim called Ray, Robby, and me into the back room.

> "Check this out."

He wrote JIM MORRISON.

"Watch this," he said with self-satisfaction.

He then began to write each letter below in a different order, crossing each out in his name, one at a time. Jim, the anagram man.

MR. MOJO RISIN

The phrase we had just recorded in "L.A. Woman"!

It is the last session of the last album the Doors will record with Jim.

On this album, *L.A. Woman*, is "The Changeling." And doesn't he confess his origins as plain as day?

> I'm a changeling, see me change,
> I'm a changeling, see me change,
> I'm the air you breathe, food you eat,
> Friends you meet in the swarming street

JAMES JAMES MORRISON MORRISON WEATHERBY GEORGE DUPREE

At first, Mojo exists as negative space. He incubates, biding his time until like the Alien he erupts, turning his host inside out, burying him in the deepest hole of creation. But for the moment James Douglas is just another pod of the wartime baby boom in Melbourne, Florida (later Cape Kennedy and Cape Canaveral). Jim's first three years are spent with his father's parents in Clearwater, Florida. (Years later, Mick Jagger and Keith Richards will write "Satisfaction" in a Clearwater motel room.)

Vivid recollections of childhood incidents. His first memory: a large room, four or five grown-ups swarm around him—huge, distorted faces, inane expressions, holding out their large meaty hands. Lumbering Brobdingnagians cooing and billing, foolishly solicitous. Competing for his attention, "Come to me, Jimmy, come to me...."

SOMEBODY GOT LUCKY BUT IT WAS AN ACCIDENT

Four years old, age of magic events. Jim has a mystical experience on the highway heading toward Santa Fe.

Outside Albuquerque, the Morrisons come upon an overturned truck. Injured and dying Pueblo Indians are strewn in the middle of the road. Phantom massacre. Custer.

As the family car pulls away from the scene of the accident, Jim feels the soul of a dead Indian enter his body and possess him. This is the cosmogonic instant, that point around which everything afterward would revolve. "The most important moment of my life," says Morrison. Demon Jim is there too, you can bet on it.

Morrison's previous biographers, being reasonable men, are ill at ease with this incident. Believers in progress, science and secular humanism, they are people who, despite five millennia of human history, still believe in…accidents!

Jim's father, too, has a hard time with the incident at Albuquerque. Finally exasperated by his son's tenacious vision, he declares that Jim has imagined the whole thing.

We, however, can believe whatever we wish, including what Jim believed: that the soul of a dying Pueblo Indian did at that instant enter his body. Is it really any more unlikely than that figment of the imagination passed on to us by a Viennese neurologist on a coke binge (the Unconscious)?

> Indians scattered on dawn's highway, bleeding ghosts crowd
> the young child's fragile,
> egg-shell mind.
>
> > "Peace Frog"

Jim's hymn to the prehistoric heart of America, the Indian.

COMING OF AGE ON THE NATIONAL PSYCHIC FAULTLINE

Morrison hatched into adolescence at a pivotal moment in American culture. World War II, delinquency, drugs, sexual promiscuity, Sinatra. Everything was changing, and it all reached a critical mass by 1955. Jim was twelve.

Enter *Rebel Without a Cause* and then the following January…Elvis! Beatniks! Action Painters! Horror movies

The band involved in a rebus-like game (the Forest of Symbols) where each Door would stand for a different letter of the alphabet. This acrostic has never been satisfactorily solved. Venice Beach, Calif., 1967. (Photograph © 1967 Bobby Klein, courtesy FAHEY/KLEIN Gallery, Los Angeles)

from Universal Studios! And, of course, James Dean, rock 'n' roll, and the ensuing fracture in American culture, the faultline.

At the root of all this was America's Teen Dream, a sort of Id-like lunge at conventional morality and the doltish adult world in general. Unfocused in the fifties, with the next generation it would dilate to cosmic proportions: the antiwar movement, sexual freedom, cosmic consciousness, civil rights, organic rice. Rock 'n' roll.

Jim felt there should be rites of passage for coming of age in America (there aren't?), called for demarcations, rituals, symbols and celebrations, and then went on to embalm his own angst in that perpetual state of adolescence: rock stardom.

ᵦ

At ten, Jim is kicked out of the Cub Scouts for sassing the den mother. A good start. Little Jim has a dark side, the watching-the-guy-drown-in-the-swamp facet of personality. A touch of domestic horror: His younger brother Andy suffers from chronic tonsillitis, making it difficult for him to breathe. Whenever this annoyed Jim, he would tape his sleeping brother's mouth shut with cellophane.

That Mojo! Always making James Douglas do those wicked things! How else, seriously, are you going to explain this? Someday, of course, someone will do a really thorough job on Jim, the conclusive psychobio that will Explain Everything. Mystery of the genes and personality, perhaps. Or maybe we could stick it on his parents. But where did they go wrong? They didn't even spank him. A nice middle-class family. Daddy a career officer in the Navy. Although, come to think of it, there *is* something a bit nutty in the old sea dog's eyes, a slightly crazed look in the official Navy photo.

Some have advanced the theory that because Jim was a Navy brat, the rootlessness of life in the military service might be the source of his compulsions. But if this were so, wouldn't the continent be swarming with precocious little damned poets? Or maybe his father didn't pay enough attention to him. Physically absent, mentally preoccupied. Playing golf at the Army/Navy Country Club. Oh dear. Mother a control freak. A domestic tyrant. Imagine the Admiral just back from the Gulf of Tonkin. The supreme commander of the biggest aircraft carrier in the world—the *Bonny Dick*—being made to take out the garbage. What a power trip!

Still, does any of this really explain that holy terror, Jeremiah Jim?

&.

The masturbation stuff from the Fud Ford Collection is classic. Fud Ford was Jim's teenage buddy. Some of these diseased extrusions were intended as commercials for the Society for the Prevention of Masturbation, and their accompanying text comes complete with puerile pseudomedical jargon ("stridopsis of the papuntasistula gland") promptly translated for the layman (as "big red prick") and a staff of ever-helpful nurses willing to offer a helping hand.

Catalogue raisonné of drawings by the pubescent Jim Morrison: man with a Coca-Cola bottle for a penis, a can opener for testicles. Fly-badgered, rotten-toothed perverts drooling over hose-length cocks, morons masturbating on one leg, a mummified Alfred E. Neuman impaled by swords, arrows and light bulbs…Dr. Freud!

Among the drawings is a presumed self-portrait and a hairy, bearded Beatnik reacting to something he sees (Jim, doing what?), with tongue hanging out and dilated eyes reacting. "Good Lord!" he says.

High school girlfriend, Tandy Martin:

> I asked him why he played games, and he said, "You'd never stay interested in me if I didn't."

Friend/classmate:

> We were so goddamned straight that when someone actually did these nervy things, things *we* wanted to do, we felt gratified in a sense, and we gravitated toward Morrison. He was a center for us.

THE ADEPT

Jim was part of the mass bohemia of the sixties. The middle class had a perverse reverence for the very people they had despised and driven to extremes. But these prisoners of suburbia now worshipped their very outcasts; sentimentalized their lives, enshrined their works, hung their art on waiting room walls. A whole generation of kids was brought up to idolize Parisian perverts, drug addicts, alcoholics and the clinically insane!

Their lives had been romanticized in novels and made into melodramas. *Lust for Life, The Agony and the Ecstasy!* It was irresistible. But most seekers of the flame could not arrange to have the crushing misfortune and abuse necessary to produce a truly radical personality such as Rimbaud or Van Gogh. Hadn't middle-class life at midcentury been deliberately designed to exclude experiences of this kind?

Yet the very blandness of suburban life provided a perfect foil for the outrages of the avant garde, which now seemed all the more flamboyant. And bourgeois life had its own horrors. Boredom, hypocrisy, philistinism, claustrophobia. Not a bad breeding ground for monsters.

Without any effort at all, a teenager of curious and defiant nature could patch into the life of, say, Vincent Van Gogh. Misunderstood, dying young and virtually unrecognized. An art of audaciousness and spiritual intensity. Van Gogh wanted his work (if not actually himself) to fuse with the elemental forces that drove the cosmic wheel. Like his friend, Paul Gauguin, Van Gogh wanted to *be* nature, to make art that would belong to nature as much as a tree or a cactus.

There's a new biography out on Van Gogh, Jim, and I'm sure glad you never got to see it, man! They say he cut off his ear because of an inner-ear infection. "The image of Vincent as isolated Holy Fool, artist-sage, or whatever has finally been exposed as the nonsense it always was." Bummer, Jim! Anyway, that's not the Vincent Van *we* grew up with, is it? Just look at the exploding face in the straw hat. That fiery spirit whirling and careening about Arles, the stars are on fire and the trees in flames, that hot pepper of modernism!

The precocious adolescent drawn to the savage grace of the doomed artist will sooner or later come across that nineteenth-century French punk from the northern provinces, Arthur Rimbaud. Rimbaud was almost certainly Jim Morrison's immaculate conception of the creative artist—cursed by Fate and thereby consecrated.

The Rimbaud legend encompasses so many irresistible elements: precocious genius, defiance, exotic places, and self-destruction (the last being the most seductive of all, the very paradigm of romantic myth). Predestined tragedy, alcoholism, madness and addiction, pain and vision!

Verlaine, Rimbaud, Baudelaire, Gérard de Nerval. Morrison looked into the lives of these *poètes maudits*, and saw his own reflection. The poet's destiny (he noted) was more than just...*scribbling words*. It was a commitment to live fast and die young, and the way one did it—with great panache—was everything.

Fever raging in one's blood! Only death could extinguish such an existential fire. Poets were not those bearded, balding, mousy professors of creative writing with tenure. They were...priests of the Invisible! Hierophants! Mirrors of gigantic shadows cast by the future on the present.

> From my ancestors, the Gauls, I get idolatry, love of sacrilege...well, all the vices, anger, lust—divine lust!— most of all lying and laziness. I hate any kind of work.
>
> The pagan blood returns! The Spirit is close... I await God ravenously...I shall come back, tough as nails, like a redskin, with ferocious eye and terrifying mask. People will say he comes from a savage tribe. I shall have gold. I will be lazy and brutal. Women dote on ferocious invalids back from the tropics.
>
> Cries, tambourines, dancing, dancing, dancing, dancing! I shall sink into nothingness.
>
> The best thing is a drunken sleep on the beach.
>
> Arthur Rimbaud, *A Season in Hell*

Like his idol, Rimbaud, Jim would go around muttering, "I alone have the key to this savage sideshow!"

And then there was Charles Baudelaire (1821–1867), the decadent dandy whose *Les Fleurs du mal* scandalized his contemporaries. A dabbler in hashish, poxy whores, and absinthe. "Epatez le bourgeois!" *My Heart Laid Bare*, written during the onset of his syphilitic insanity, is the very testament of the tormented artist.

> I have cultivated my hysteria with delight and terror. Now I suffer constantly from vertigo, and today, 23rd of January, 1862, I have received a singular warning. I have felt the wind of the wing of madness pass over me.

The two cardinal texts of the *poètes maudits* are Rimbaud's letter to Paul Demeny and Baudelaire's poem "Enivrez vous!" Rimbaud's manifesto, known as *Le Voyant*, goes something like this: To be a great poet, kid, you must first get *out there!* Stop making sense! Suffer! Madness, baby, mad-ness! If it says poison, well, that's just to stop you from getting into the good stuff. Give in to temptation, baby, that's what it's there for! Oh, and put a hole in your soul. Also, repeat after me, "I is another, I is another...."

In the second dictum of Decadence (Baudelaire's "Get High!") the gist is: Get as wrecked as you can on anything you can lay your hands on—coffee, yage, cigarettes, junk food, grass, acid, booze, sugar rush, ibogaine, late night TV. The more out of it you get, the more into *it* you'll be, dig? Never come down. The mayor's getting high, why shouldn't I? Be unreasonable. Deny everything. Whatever it is...just say yes!

Jim Morrison, the aesthetosaur, son of a career Navy officer, read these ancient manifests and took them to heart. Every high is the same high, every form of love the same, every book the same book. Coleridge, De Quincy, all those opium-dabbling English Romantics. Maybe Borges. This was heady stuff.

And just as he was reading about all these frenzied *fin de siècle* French madmen and geniuses, thinking that he had

"He's really an artist...The sound waves are his canvas, the group is his brush...Then he puts himself into the center of it and becomes part of his art. It frames him and he IS and CREATES at the same time." *Crawdaddy.* Kennedy Stadium, Bridgeport, Conn., 1968. (Photograph by Tom Hammang)

been born too late, had missed out…right then, out there in San Francisco, on Venice Beach, in Greenwich Village, on the road…it was all happening again. Hairy, mystical, pot-smoking, free-loving freeloaders. Beatniks!

September 1957. The Morrisons move to Alameda, California. Jim, age fourteen, picks up Jack Kerouac's *On the Road*. The Signet paperback blurb reads:

> The Zen Barbarians
>
> Pod…Jazz…Zen: these are the boosters of the Beat Generation. Sal Paradise…Dean Moriarty: these are the reckless, riotous, nonviolent revolutionaries who hunger after Life, Experience, Sensation, Truth. *On the Road* is the explosive chronicle of two youths' refusal to bow to authority, to conform to a society they cannot accept.…Wild drives across America…wrecking cars…picking up girls, making love, all-night drinking bouts, jazz joints, wild parties, hot spots.

But this wasn't just something out of the past, something you could only fantasize about. It all was happening right now in the USA. In the most overblown era of American history, Romanticism was back with a vengeance. Pollock, Ginsberg, Kerouac, Michael McClure, Gregory Corso. They had read all this stuff, too. Rimbaud's letter to Paul Demeny, Baudelaire's declaration of decadence on their GI Bill of Rights grants.

IQ 149. Jim's taste in reading is so arcane that his English teacher does a Library of Congress check to see if the books he is reporting on actually exist.

Self-portraits as Jim the King. Posing as Alexander the Great. The first famous person in history. What a role model! Inclination of head toward left shoulder.

Jim begins keeping a journal, writing poetry. At first, cowboy ballads ("The Pony Express"). "Horse Latitudes" (written during his senior year in high school) is elegantly cryptic and cinematic. It will eventually be used as a lyric on the Doors' second album, *Strange Days*.

Southern Californian vegetation deity in Muir Woods, Marin County, Calif., 1967. (Photograph © 1967 Bobby Klein, courtesy FAHEY/KLEIN Gallery, Los Angeles)

To his mother—a fine thing!—"You sound like a pig when you eat."

24 FANTASIES PER SECOND

Eighteenth birthday. Balcony walking (drunk) twenty feet above the ground. First the attitude, then those decadent foreigners and Beatniks, the manifestos, the direct commands to debauchery and the ensuing malaise. Jim's spirits rising. Heavy drinking. By his senior year he is cynical, bitter, obsessive. Mojo beginning to take hold.

Jim begins telling people he has *it*. Just like Elvis (and Alexander the Great). A spiritual substance that can be magically transferred to anything he put his hands on. He has only to choose!

Alan Rhodes, owner of the Renaissance Hotel, a bar Jim frequents, gives him some showbiz advice: "Show your meat—never knew it to fail."

Fall 1961. Jim attends Florida State University. A course in the philosophy of protest: Montaigne, Hume, Sartre, Heidegger. His favorite is Nietzsche. John Densmore would later say, "Nietzsche killed Jim Morrison."

He writes a paper called "The Sexual Neuroses of Crowds." It is the germ of Jim's conception of the performer as healer, the shaman who can draw out evil spirits and banish them. Crowds, like people, have diseases that can be diagnosed and treated. This is an idea that he may have absorbed from the French incendiary, madman and theoretician of drama, Antonin Artaud (*The Theater and Its Double*).

According to Gestalt psychology, the mob has a collective psyche. Jim saw large groups of people as personifications, like Thomas Hobbes' awesome image of Leviathan, the composite entity. The mobmind of Isaac Asimov's *Foundation and Empire*:

> Psycho-history dealt not with man, but with man-masses. It
> was the science of mobs....It could forecast reactions to
> stimuli with something of the accuracy that a lesser science

Jim: "I offer images—I conjure memories of freedom...We can only open doors—we can't drag people through." Magic Mountain outdoor concert, Marin County, Calif., 1967. (Photograph by Gene Anthony)

could bring to the forecast of a rebound of a billiard ball. The reaction of one man could be forecast by no known mathematics; the reaction of a billion is something else again.

The study of crowds would be Jim's lifelong pursuit. It was the mastery of this science that would, ironically, lead to his downfall:

> I can look at a crowd, I can just look at it, it's all, uh, very scientific and I can diagnose the crowd psychologically. Just four of us properly positioned can turn the crowd around. We can *cure* it. We can *make love to it*. We can make it *riot*.

Nurtured on a midcentury American diet of movies, TV commercials and the evening news, Jim didn't much distinguish between direct and indirect experience, or fantasy and reality, for that matter. Letters to his parents about imaginary events. The one about getting people to exit quietly from the theater he would later on reverse with a vengeance.

Jim's brother, Andy:

> He wouldn't write about dates or anything. He'd tell a story. About how he was at a movie theater when a fire broke out and everybody panicked and stormed the doors, and he was the only one who remained calm. He got up on the stage, sat at the piano and sang a song, and calmed the audience so that they exited from the theater safely. Another letter was filled with details about how he watched a guy drown in a swamp.

❧

January 1964. Jim attends UCLA Film School. His intention is to translate his fantasies into film. At that time the faculty includes Stanley Kramer, Jean Renoir, Josef Von Sternberg. Francis Ford Coppola is a student, as is the Doors' future keyboard player, Ray Manzarek.

Like two other exhibitionist intellectuals (and fellow Celts), Oscar Wilde and Bernard Shaw, Jim has a long apprenticeship. This includes college, film school, reading, and developing an aphoristic, paradoxical style that will come to dazzle the press with its startling, infectious coinings.

Jim's multifaceted education also includes fascination with

Jim: "Pain is meant to wake us up. People try to hide from pain. But they're wrong. Pain is something to carry, like a radio." Old Minneapolis Auditorium, Minneapolis, Minn., 1968. (Photograph by Mike Barich)

the bizarre and grotesque: freaks and cripples at the Lucky U, an off-campus Mexican restaurant and bar, blind men pushing legless friends around in wheelchairs, lady bartenders and whores. (This taste for low life has a long literary precedent.) Drunken trip to Mexico. Bar to bar. Talking to pimps, dealers, hermaphrodite bartenders, hookers in boozy Mexican cantinas. Chased by dogs. Just as in Malcolm Lowry's *Under the Volcano.* The Mexican, Aztec horror-humor thing with death, the *calaveras,* skeletons miming every conceivable human activity.

Jim saw himself as a misfit much in the tradition of Colin Wilson's *The Outsider.* Wilson was a precocious compiler whose book expounded the beyond-the-pale role of the creative artist in a hostile and philistine society. *The Outsider* was extremely popular among students and disaffected youth of the fifties, a veritable malcontent's primer for outcasts. Jim identified with freaks in the same way that Kerouac had identified with the felaheen of the world, the downtrodden, the peasant, the beaten down.

But Jim Morrison didn't look like a freak. He seemed, if anything, the very antithesis of abnormal. He was the ideal, the criterion, the enticement, the guy in the ad that you get (or get to be) if you buy the product. He's the guy driving the Ferrari.

Hence, Jim's identification with the suffering, persecuted artist is somewhat quirky. (As if Cheryl Tiegs were to develop an obsessive identification with Gertrude Stein.)

Jim identified with Rimbaud, but Rimbaud was a goofy-looking, pimply, tormented nineteenth-century homosexual, plagued by fire and brimstone, pursued by terrifying images of eternal damnation from a fanatical catholicism. Rimbaud's mother, a zealously devout peasant, put her children in coffins and lowered them into open graves to impress on them the hell fire of repentance.

Whereas Jim had a nice, normal middle-class upbringing. He was exceptionally handsome, charming and intelligent. He had few money problems. In a way it was hard to believe that someone who looked that good had ever had *any* problems, let alone actually suffered.

So Jim's life as a doomed poet will always seem a little like a movie about the life of Rimbaud, typically miscast in the traditional Hollywood manner. Don't miss Jim Morrison in *A Season in Hell!* To get across the life of a tormented artist, you cast a dreamboat as the lead. Trust me.

All those demented, possessed, persecuted artists and poets that Jim identified with had grudges against society. They were outcasts. People *literally* cast them out, threw them in gutters. And their afflictions often had little to do with their calling. They were not spat upon, humiliated and dismissed because they were poets or painters. Indeed, for the most part their creations were simply ignored. These Symbolist saints were persecuted because they were social pariahs—branded in some way, disfigured.

Alienation had fueled the art of the *poètes maudits;* their works could be seen as a form of revenge, a personal attack upon a world that had rejected them. But Doomed Jim's identification with outcasts seemed an unmotivated, even idealistic choice.

He had no demonstrable reason for being embittered, doomy, misanthropic. He was famous. He was rich. Women threw themselves at him. Intellectuals and rock literati made fools of themselves coining epithets for him. Socialites and other famous people contended with one another to have him to dinner (a serious mistake). What was the matter with him? He had everything, yet he persisted in tearing it all down. So adolescent of him!

Even compared with such peers as Jimi Hendrix and Janis Joplin, Morrison seemed to somehow fit in. Jimi and Janis were true freaks: a psychedelic black who played to white audiences, and an overweight Southern "Beatnik chick" with skin problems who had once been voted "Ugliest Man on Campus." Not even from the Midwest, Morrison was a Middle American messiah. Janis, Jimi, Dylan—all were fringe. Morrison was by nature more like James Dean. Not quite a freak, but born to be wild.

Jim: "We're like actors—turned loose in this world to wander in search of a phantom." Felt Form, Madison Square Garden, New York, N.Y., March, 1970. (Photograph by Joseph Sia)

FOLLOWING SPREAD
LEFT

"Barbie speaks when we pull her string....that's why we want him to sing "Light My Fire" and stop stop STOP all these other strange sentences that the doll didn't say when we bought her." Liza Williams. Portland, Oreg., 1968. (Photograph by Andrew Kent Hall)

RIGHT

Jim: "It's that old thing like a first novel, they usually give the cat a break, everybody kind of pats him on the back. And the second one, they really chop him up." Portland, Oreg., 1968. (Photograph by Douglas Kent Hall)

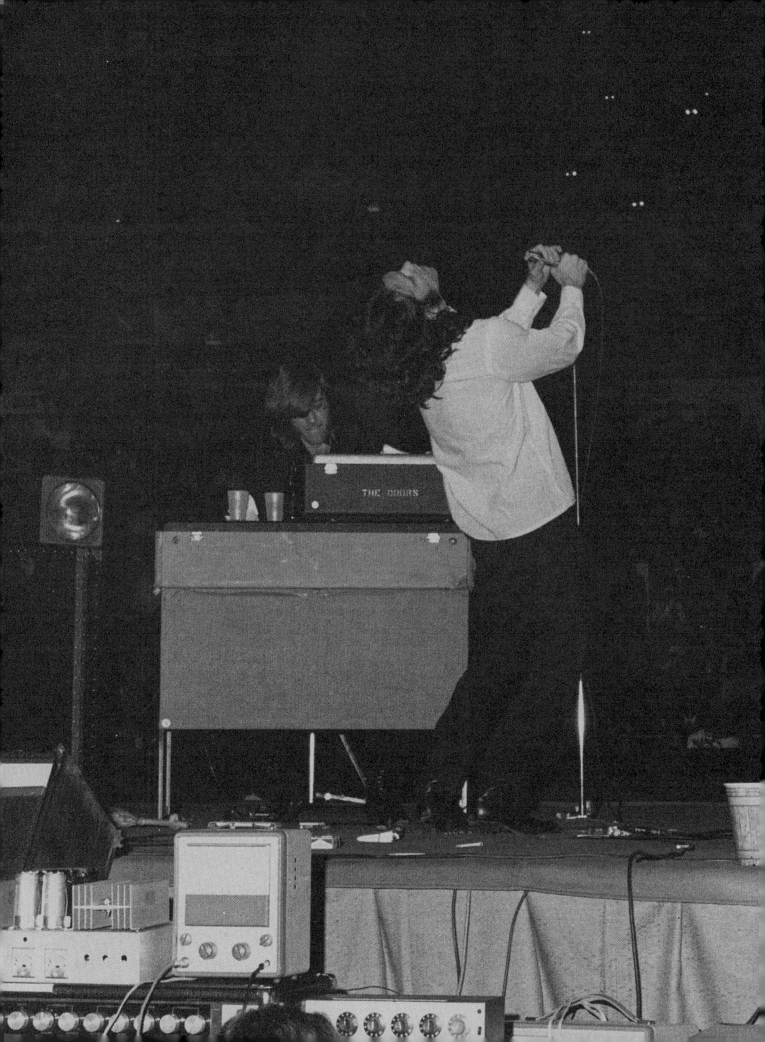

Even now in college, Jim is pissing in the library stacks. Drunk, rowdy, rolling empty wine bottles down the aisles, daredevilry, climbing campus towers, stripping off clothes. Quasimodo without the deformities.

❧

Spring 1965. Jim and fellow film school student Dennis Jakob plan to form a band called the Doors: Open and Closed.

He develops an interest in shamanism, the poet inspired, the healer, the magus. He sees the origins of cinema in magic, sorcery, the "summoning of phantoms." This interest in the occult power of art—not as something to contemplate from afar, but as a means of transforming the audience—is at the heart of most twentieth-century revolutions in aesthetics. Picasso's *Demoiselles d'Avignon* insists on the magical, demonic origins of representation, just as the fragment in Rainer Maria Rilke's poem "Archaic Torso of Apollo" makes demands on the viewer that transcend aesthetics:

> We will never know his ancient thoughts
> or what those buried eyes have seen.
> And yet his torso still radiates an archaic presence
> smoldering with all its ferocity beneath the marble.
> If this were not so…
>
> how would you explain the inexhaustible light that
> beaming from its every particle like an exploding star
> penetrates to the core of your being?
> Or why its terrible eyes are still shouting:
> You must change your life!

The insistence that a work of art somehow transform the audience would become the guiding principle of Jim's career as a performer. Paradoxically, the primacy of art as an active principle in life meant that the boundaries between the real and imaginary could be abolished. It no longer mattered. "You blur the distinction between dreams and reality," because, to quote his classmate John DeBella, "dreams begat reality":

We had a theory of the True Rumor. Life wasn't as excit-
ing and romantic as it should be, so you tell things that are
false because it is better that images be created. It doesn't
matter that they aren't true, so long as they're believed.

Jim: "With an image there's no attendant danger."
Oh yeah?

ða.

Jim's first student project is typical: a film questioning the
film process itself. He also plans to do the life of Rimbaud,
then the scene in Nietzsche's life where he runs into the
street to restrain a man from whipping a horse (the horror
of which eventually brought on Nietzsche's madness). In
the end Jim's film is oddly prophetic, prefiguring his own
future as sexual shaman and erotic politician. He splices
together jump-cut sequences from a psych film showing a
man and woman nude simulating sex against a track of
Ravel's *Bolero*.

In his "Notes on Vision"—in *The Lords,* his first book of
poetry—Jim played with the idea of the voyeur, the
Peeping Tom as an alienated joker whose menace and
power come from his collusion with his prey, a concept that
would permeate his lyrics: the eye as weapon.

Jim cultivates an aesthete's morbid sensibility. Images of
madness, sex, death, randomness, nihilism, fury and melancholy thrill him. Self-mutilation, self-degradation, auto-
damnation. A student's intoxication, but few accumulate
such an extensive catalog of the grotesque. *Amour de la boue.*
Jim identifies with the suffering Dionysus in Nietzsche's
Birth of Tragedy. But, as Nietzsche observed, if one looks
into the abyss, the abyss looks back into one's own spirit. So
it comes as no surprise that Jim is developing a sense of
apprehension. Things are getting out of control.

Captain Steve Morrison (Dad) in Gulf of Tonkin incident
off Vietnam. Again wins annual officers' push-up contest.

Everything Solid Melts into Air.

James Dean, Elvis, Jackson Pollock, Jack Kerouac. An idea was beginning to form in a few fitful heads that you could be famous, famous in the sense of mass popularity, and still make art. The equation of art + fame + Popness (Popness = fame *now!*) was a fantasy that many dreamed about so fiercely that it came true.

When *Time* magazine said about Kerouac "he writes like a literary James Dean," a spark flew out into the world. *Time* magazine! The idea that you could make art that was instantaneously popular was irresistible to precocious adolescents in the fifties. And so American! The very essence of Democracy, the systole of its tricolor heart.

James Dean was the epitome of Pop in his combination of youth, fame, genius and life style. He had somehow got around the supposed contradiction between art and popularity. And unlike his predecessors Montgomery Clift and Marlon Brando, he had no disdain for the movies as a crass medium for mass entertainment.

Out there, where they had never heard of Rimbaud or Baudelaire, they read *Time* magazine in the barber shops, bus stations and doctors' waiting rooms. And all of them (Bob Dylan, Jimi Hendrix, Lou Reed, Andy Warhol, Janis Joplin, Jack Nicholson and…Jim Morrison) at some point or other picked up that most despised of capitalist rags, and saw an article about these wild artists, Jack Kerouac and Jackson Pollock. Even through the heavy gauze of sneery

Have have have you you you ever ever ever tried tried tried to to to sing sing sing on on on acid? acid? acid? Felt Form, Madison Square Garden, New York, N.Y., March, 1970. (Photograph by Jason Lauré/Woodfin Camp)

Lucespeak ("Jack the Dripper") you, if you were a sensitive teenager stuck out in some suburban compound or inner-city tenement, you knew at once These Men Were Titans.

The very scorn *Time* and its loathesome twin, *Newsweek,* poured on these geniuses only confirmed their greatness. Artists in *Time* magazine! Like movie stars.... Artists starring in a movie about themselves! The plot, the lines, the art, the life style—all their own creation. There wasn't yet a word for what they were doing, but French film buffs would soon call the I-did-it-all-myself movie director an *auteur.* The description would apply to the new Pop art as well, for stars were now the authors of their own lives.

And it was not long before some of the kids who'd been reading about those great big angelic geniuses began to think about doing the same thing themselves, not in books or on canvas but in popular music.

There had, of course, been geniuses in Pop music before this, although nobody except musicologists and booking agents ever called them artists. Louis Armstrong, Charlie Parker, Robert Johnson, Hank Williams, Howling Wolf—even Elvis—intuitive geniuses all.

European High Modernist painters and poets paid tribute to them—whiff of condescension of the Broadway Boogie Woogie variety—but the musicians themselves did not think of what they did as art in the tradition of High Modernist aesthetics. They didn't think about High Modernist aesthetics; mainly they thought about getting high.

This only made the Bop 'n' Pop idols all the more exemplary (they were a force of nature) in the eyes of a new generation of elite bohemians like Dylan, Hendrix and Morrison. These giants (the jazz greats, the blues demons) grew out of the earth, out of the folk. Their power came from the mad, wild wisdom of the blood, an ancient chthonic source.

But Jim Morrison—like Dylan, Jagger and Joplin—did not come from a tradition of blues and jazz oral poets and griots. They didn't come from a tradition of much of any-

He who once sailed with Drake and Magellan, stranded in a strange port, sweaty, sexy, sultry, and buzzed, now sings to sailors, sirens, and the sons of semi-conductor czars. Old Minneapolis Auditorium, Minneapolis, Minn., 1968. (Photograph by Mike Barich)

thing. They weren't *poètes maudits* either, outside of their imaginations.

They couldn't even choose to be pure 100% Pop, like Elvis or Sinatra, because that state of being itself came from a mysteriously crass folk strength that excluded choice. They couldn't choose to be mere entertainers any more than they could choose to become Druse prophets. They hadn't been born that way; they were middle class. Their choices seemed infinite, but nothing was real.

❧

Nevertheless (just when things appeared bleakest) a new synthesis presented itself, one which would combine all these elements—the blooze, the doomed poet, the artist writing his own movie and the musician reading about same—and this was sixties rock. Like everything great in American culture, it was all in the blend. So when these teen protobohemians came of age, they began to brew various mixes of popular music into new formulations that included as many elements of their fantasy as possible.

One of these concoctions was dreamed up by two ex-film school students, Ray Manzarek and Jim Morrison. It involved a mix of rock, blues, avant garde theater, fun house surrealism, Symbolist verse and film technique. Around this overarching concept, the Doors came into being. Ray:

> We tried to marry poetry and music much in the same
> manner of the poetry and jazz of the Beatnik era, the fifties
> and early sixties. We tried to do poetry and rock 'n' roll.

The Doors were also a strange brew of contrasting temperaments. Ray essentially sunny, Panglossian, balanced, Utopian, ironic, sanguine. Jim *Sturm und Drang*, possessed, melancholic, demonic, intense, fatalistic. Their Manichean polarity was essential to the nature of the Doors. Tension, contrast, figure and ground. They were the two representative types of artist defined by Nietzsche: the artist who imitates dreams and the artist who imitates drunkenness.

Jim and Ray had a vision of rock 'n' roll that had inex-

Okay, that's Ray on the right, obviously, and that must be me [Jim] over on the left. Jesus, but who are those other guys? I've got to lay off the booze, man, this is getting embarrassing. Old Minneapolis Auditorium, Minneapolis, Minn., 1969. (Photograph by Mike Barich)

haustible possibilities. Rock was something that was just emerging, that had happened in their lifetime. Like film, born earlier in the century, there were no rules. According to Jim:

> The good thing about film is that there aren't any experts. There's no authority on film. Anyone can assimilate and contain the whole history of film in himself, which you can't do in other arts. There are no experts, so any student knows almost as much as any professor.

Okay, let's reinvent the wheel!

DHARMA BUM ON VENICE BEACH

Meanwhile…out there in California, in an old bohemian colony, Venice Beach, the hero of our story is transforming himself. Shedding his old skin, he is becoming a bum, drifting, plucking things out of the air, getting high.

1965, 1966—Jim's years in the desert. A prophet "howling in the Wilderness against a crazy civilization" (Ginsberg's description of the Beats). In the classic American tradition of self-invention—like Huck Finn lighting out for the territory, Dean Moriarty on the road—he strives to erase his past and start over again, tabula rasa.

Jim never gave up his vagabondage. He had a total disregard for money, never carried a wallet, and, unless someone found a place for him to stay, rarely had a bed of his own. When he did, he often could not remember where it was, and ended up sleeping on old ladies' doorsteps or even on the couches of total strangers (where he mistakenly had asked to be driven home). Whether people recognized the disheveled *divus* curled up on their rug or whether they were simply charmed, cajoled, or too stunned to refuse him, these are hosts familiar from folklore. The king has lost his way in the forest and is taken in by a poor woodcutter.

Jim could be extremely charming (that Cheshire cat smile). Women found him irresistible. They put him up, fed him ("Soul Kitchen" is dedicated to Olivia's soul food restaurant in Venice Beach, where Jim could always get free meals), acted as booking agents, publicists, *wahinis*, nannies…whatever.

Living on a rooftop in Venice Beach, taking a lot of acid ("10,000 mikes" was all he said), writing in his journal songpoems about death, insanity.

Air conditioning, TV antennas, tiny rooms….Most of these notebooks Jim eventually burned on a subsequent acid trip. One of the poems that survived was used as the lyric to "Cars Hiss by My Window" on the Doors' last album.

Reading the Beats and the grisly giants of French modernism, that euphonic flock of names: Apollinaire, Char, Desnos, Daumal, Reverdy, Michaux, Cendrars, Ponge, Quineau, Prévert….A line from French rat-tat-tat-telegraphic novelist Louis Ferdinand Céline's epic, *Journey to the End of the Night* ("take the highway to the end of the night"), becomes the title for Jim's first song, "End of the Night."

❧

A book Jim borrowed from the UCLA library informs us that spiders on acid produce geometric designs; on mescaline, random, chaotic ones. Jim's reaction: "Let's go try some of that!"

Minting the maxims with which he will soon stun interviewers: "There's the known and the unknown and then there's the door between them. That's what I want to be." (Later, variously ascribed to William Blake and Ray Manzarek.)

He had a conjurer's code: long periods of practice and incubation followed by…*what next!* This gathering, sifting and Bardo gazing all contribute to the astonishing impact of the Doors' first album. Also to the origins of a number of Doors songs from this period: "Hello, I Love You," "Moonlight Drive," "Soul Kitchen," "My Eyes Have Seen You," "The End."

Fateful meeting with Pamela Courson. Doe-eyed, hippie child woman. They are inseparable (in their fashion) for the rest of his life. He calls her his "cosmic mate." She calls herself "Jim's creation."

Jim runs into Ray Manzarek again on the beach. This is Ray's description of their encounter:

> It was 1965 and it was summer and we had graduated. School was finished. We had to do something. What are you going to do with your life? Two months later, sometime in July, sittin' out here on the beach in Venice, and who comes walking down the beach but Jim Morrison. I said hey, man, I thought you'd gone to New York. He said no I decided to stay here. I was writing some songs and living up on Dennis Jakob's rooftop. So I said listen, let me hear one of the songs. Can you sing one for me? So he sat down on the beach and he said here's one I got... "Moonlight Drive."
>
> And when I heard the first lines, man, I said wow, that's it. Best lyrics I've ever heard for a rock 'n' roll song!
>
> Let's swim to the moon, uh huh
> Let's climb through the tide
> Penetrate the evening that the
> City sleeps to hide.

Ray plays keyboards in a club band called Rick and the Ravens, with his brothers Rick and Jim on guitars and harmonica. He recruits jazz drummer John Densmore to form a group. They call themselves the Doors. William Blake presides at their baptism.

> If the doors of perception were cleansed,
> everything would appear to man as it is, infinite.
>
> William Blake, *The Marriage of Heaven and Hell*

This was the line that inspired the title of Aldous Huxley's drug log, *The Doors of Perception*.

Jim tells his parents of his intention to form rock band. (His father reminds him of the time he refused to join family caroling.) The group plays small clubs, and gradually puts together a six-song demo tape. (Billy James, a talent scout for Columbia Records, signs the Doors to a short-term contract which eventually lapses.)

The contraposto of a Renaissance statue, the melancholy aspect of a Romantic poet, the aura of decadence fuse together. Kennedy Stadium, Bridgeport, Conn., 1968. (Photograph by Tom Hammang)

THE CRYSTAL SHIP IS BEING FILLED

Soon Ray's brothers quit, and Robby Krieger, a jug band guitarist who had played with John in a group called the Psychedelic Rangers, replaces them. The Doors are complete. Drums, guitar, electric organ, lead singer.

They are still looking for a bass player, but most of the bass players they rehearse give them a sound that is too full— a sound, in any case, that had already been well exploited, most notably by the Rolling Stones. They are anxious to distinguish themselves from the Stones, since much of what they play at the time is blues. They also do many of the same songs ("Little Red Rooster," for instance).

The solution comes when Ray discovers the Fender Rhodes keyboard bass, which he can control with his left hand while playing chords and solos with his right on the Vox organ. Now they've got the sound down. The ironic counterpoint of Ray's organ to Jim's portentous lyrics. John's jazzy, punctuating drumming. Robby's eclectic guitar. A generalized, creamy, soft-focus, swoony sound alternating with a ferocious, V-8 engine—that Fender Rhodes keyboard bass. A hurdy-gurdy tinniness, fugal jet modalities, engines whirring, generators humming, the sonic grammar of appliances, of things turned on.

John Milius, screenwriter of *Apocalypse Now*: "When I want some good pagan carnage, I put on the Doors."

Then there's Jim's voice. One of the great voices in rock, it could swing unexpectedly between a loutish croon and a blues bellow. "I don't sing," he said, "I shout." His own appraisal of his voice in the poem "Making Records" was quite brutal. Compared with Elvis's sex-wise voice, he thinks of his own as that of a repressed teenager. *A scream or a sick croon. Nothing in between.*

Few bands had as eccentric a way of composing and arranging their material as the Doors. Acidhead songwriting séances. Ray: "We'd listen to Jim chant-sing the words over and over and the sound that should go with them would slowly emerge."

Another method became more common as time went on and Jim's disappearances became more frequent. It involved a reverse procedure in which the band would set up a rhythmic environment into which Jim (when he finally showed in the studio) would read/sing/croon/shout lyrics he'd written, sometimes neatly typed on foolscap, but sometimes taken directly from his notebooks, soggy napkins or matchbook covers. These funkograms already had a rhythmic pulse so they easily clicked onto the tune.

The never-is-heard-a-discouraging-word aspect of the Doors' relationship to Jim is remarkable considering what he must have put them through. They seem always to be in sync, even in the outer reaches of indulgent behavior and random, impulsive craziness on the part of the lead singer.

Ray spoke of the intuition musicians develop who've played together for long periods of time, but he added that with the Doors "there was also an unusual *intensity*." Acid was the glue, according to Ray, that created the group's "communal mind." (Before the alkaloids in LSD were isolated, the mixture of chemicals that constituted the active principle was called *telepathine,* allegedly—as they say in textbooks—because of its capacity to induce extrasensory perception.)

It was cosmic, man, so naturally the Buddha, Shiva and the Tao play a part in all this. John, Robby and Ray were all into various forms of Buddhist and Hindu mysticism, meditation, mantras and yoga early on, and it was through these connections that the band met.

Not Jim, of course, a thoroughgoing pagan who, when questioned by busybodies about the vulgarity of the concluding lines of "The End," used to say, "Hey, it's my mantra, man. Fuck-the-mother-kill-the-father! Fuck-the-mother-kill-the-father...." John Densmore:

> He really wanted to get out of himself, totally go to the ends as far as you can go every time. Find out! I never understood because I came from the Indian side of metaphysics, the bright side, whatever. He was into Nietzsche and the what-does-it-all-mean and existential exploration.

The Doors were the Crystal Ship, a vessel that encapsulated them, their group soul. In *The Soul of the White Ant,* Belgian anthropoentomologist, morphine addict and visionary Eugene Marais developed a theory of psychological swarming based on his study of termite communities. Certain insect colonies constituted collective beings and functioned as "group souls."

Like the children in *Village of the Damned,* the Doors synchronized an ability to "direct their energies inward toward each other" (Ray), an ability that allowed them to digress into the uncharted regions of Meredith Monk–Sun Ra–Living Theater experiments and still tune in flawlessly in order to create those oscillating emotional ripple effects that bend their songs through eerie transformations. "The End," for instance, begins as a song about a disintegrating love affair and transmogrifies into a full-blown Oedipal psychodrama. Or "End of the Night," where William Blake's incantatory lines modulate into Céline's dark vision.

SEANCES ON THE STRIP

Jim Morrison was a perfect distillation of his time. And place. The apocalyptic Angelos out there in the desert, in the little clubs along the Strip, had been waiting a long time for their messiah to come, when (as if by destiny!) the Lizard King appeared among them. The Brits had the Stones and the Who. The East Coast had its dark princes— Dylan, Hendrix, the Velvet Underground. San Francisco, its Bardo bohemians. When is our saint due?

And there he was! Materialized, as it were, out of pentecostal Pop longing, a Renaissance statue come to life, the body of an adolescent god mailed in leather, so tight it looked as if his lithe, lanky body had simply been dipped in india ink.

No one ever caught the hallucinated, under the volcano, neon black sun vision of L.A. like Jim Morrison did. It could all vanish, and you'd only have to feed those tracks—"L.A. Woman," "Strange Days," etc.—into the holographic

Jim: "I think of myself as an intelligent, sensitive human being with the soul of a clown which always forces me to blow it at the most important moments." Bridgeport, Conn., 1968. (Photograph by Joseph Sia)

transformer to have the whole place back, right there in all its seedy, phantasmagoric beauty. Jim:

> This city is looking for a ritual to join its fragments. The Doors are looking for such a ritual, too—a sort of electric wedding.

January 1966. The Doors get a job at London Fog, a small club on Sunset Strip next to Whiskey à Go Go.

DOORS—BAND FROM VENICE reads the marquee. It might just as honestly have said:

THE DOORS
PERFORMING THE GOLDEN BOUGH
NIGHTLY! LIVE! ON STAGE!

See the Fisher King draw rain out of an industrial sky! Oedipus, Theseus and the Minotaur, Alexander the Great, the Unknown Soldier, the Ancient Snake, Endless Night, ladies and gentlemen, see them all right here. *Caballero existencialista*, Jeem!

In the hallucinated darkness of the club, Lord Jim of the American Night invokes the cave primeval, the psychosexual Cabinet of Dr. Sigismundus, an attic out of which, as in a Goya etching, bats fly. The bats are his thoughts. Bad thoughts. Reason is asleep. Reason is the reasonable, the silent majority that has fallen asleep during a commercial on the Johnny Carson show while a demonic Pied Piper steals their children's souls. "All the children are insane." (All that is sacred will be profaned.)

The Doors are conjurers of dark tableaux ("Weird scenes inside the gold mine") in the same way that during the French Revolution actors, at climactic points in the drama, would pose in *tableaux vivants* of Jean-Louis David's famous pictures. They would mimic the figures in the *Oath of the Horatii*, just as in the painting.

Doors' performances were like a series of (what else?) film clips. Slow fades, jump cuts. Freeze-frame stills. Noirish sequences. Jim's leather pants were his personal shadow, his cloud in trousers that followed him like that of the man

Do not adjust your set. Mojo brooding, backstage at the Avalon Ballroom, San Francisco, Calif., 1967. (Photograph © 1967 Bobby Klein, courtesy FAHEY/KLEIN Gallery, Los Angeles)

FOLLOWING SPREAD

Jim, Robby, John and Ray at the Lucky U Cafe in West L.A., Calif., where Jim used to hang out while a student at UCLA Film School, 1966. (Photograph © 1967 Bobby Klein, courtesy FAHEY/KLEIN Gallery, Los Angeles)

who sewed his shadow to himself. The Doors' producer, Paul Rothchild:

> The Doors brought their theater from a film view of theater. It was broader, deeper, more psychologically oriented than the rat-tat-tat-tah of the English music hall. The Doors were one of the very first American groups to appreciate very personal entertainment. It was very deep, sometimes dark, just as Jim and the other Doors liked the darker directors of film.

&

At the Fog, the theater of "The End" begins to evolve. John Densmore develops his "shamanistic drumming."

The club's clientele consists of deviates, pimps, whores, gangsters and tourists. (They don't make audiences like that anymore.) To two recent film school graduates this suggests a smoky, decadent, art deco cabaret in Weimar Berlin. So as part of their project of developing as an Art Rock quartet, the Doors include in their repertoire "Alabama Song," from the 1927 German expressionist opera *Mahagonny*. Almost no one in the audience is likely to recognize the source. Can you imagine the bizarreness, had you never heard a Bertolt Brecht/Kurt Weill song, as this strange chant comes lurching at you from some entirely alien plane of existence? Written by some extraterrestrial songwriting machine on the theme of an imaginary country called America. Jim pronounces "Alabama" as if he had never heard the word before.

"Alabama Song" is for the Doors a scene from a historical movie with a mad celeste player. Its framing of a song already in deep quotation marks makes you see the cocktail jazz element in other Doors' songs in a different light. The schmaltz becomes an artifact.

But Alabama is only the first stop in a time- and space-warped geography. There is "The End," which had begun innocently enough as the Doors' encore at the Whiskey and stretched into a molten fresco of travel-weary faces and images. A broken-off love affair, rejection, a bad trip—all seem to trigger off accumulating detonations that finally reach critical mass in the last section. "C'mon, baby, take a chance with us," Jim cajoles, summoning up terrors real and imagined, all pulsing with phosphorescence and decay. The music ebbs and swells flawlessly in sync with Shaman Jim's psychotic trance. (The organ at the climax exultantly chiming "The freaks are loose!")

Even in its early incarnations "The End" was weird enough ("take the snake to the lake," etc.) but then one night, recalls John:

> He was in his room and he wouldn't come out. So we kinda…come on, Jim….And he finally let us in. And he was under the bed and had taken a lot of acid and encouraging us to take acid. And we're going, we got a gig y'know, let's….We got him over to the Whiskey and we're doing "The End" and he threw in the Oedipal section. Got very quiet. I think we were fired that night.

"The End" is an allegorical drama of numbing naiveté whose meaning the storyteller has neglected (some might say, mercifully) to elaborate. A Symbolist drama in which the actors portray abstract ideas, feelings, theories.

The nakedness of the symbolism is both emotionally dauntless and excruciatingly embarrassing.

Many have found "The End" a bit too verbatim. The sort of raw, unchewed Freudian theory that is meant to *underlie* our chaotic and tormented lives, not serve as its text. But this apparently underestimates Jim who, according to Paul Rothchild, never thought of this sequence as anything *but* symbolic. Rothchild:

> Jim kept saying over and over kill the father, fuck the mother, and essentially it boils down to this, kill all those things in yourself which are instilled in you and are not of yourself, they are alien concepts which are not yours, they must die. The psychedelic revolution. Fuck the mother is very basic, and it means get back to the essence, what is reality, what is, fuck the mother is very basically mother, mother-birth, real, you can touch it, it's nature, it can't lie to you. So what Jim says at the end of the Oedipus section, which is essentially the same thing as the classic says, kill the alien concepts, get back to reality, the end of alien concepts, the beginning of personal concepts.

Still others have been uncomfortable with the temperamental explicitness of this piece. As with much of the Doors' material, there are no emotional stops. The distance felt to be essential to art has collapsed, the emotions are pumped up, unmediated, the sentiments portentous and overblown. The traumatic effect of the climax of "The End" depends on an almost too direct connection between infantile sexuality and mythical thinking.

As the emblematic Child Jim tiptoes stealthily along the hallway carpet, lightning flashes turn various familiar objects into fetishes of totemic dread. The looming door to the parents' bedroom opens and the veil of the temple is ripped revealing...the Primal Scene, directed by Alfred Hitchcock, with sets by Salvador Dali, and Admiral Morrison as the Minotaur.

Sex, humiliation, human sacrifice, mystery, horror, seduction....

Later, one of the blessings/misfortunes visited upon this hothouse Freudian melodrama was to be its use as a soundtrack in Francis Ford Coppola's film *Apocalypse Now*, forever linking it with an unintentional video of indelible beauty and horror. It now seems to be all about Vietnam. Oedipus at Dien Bien Phu.

❧

The Whiskey à Go Go was an ideal space for the Doors to practice their alchemical plays. A median between private and public space where they could experiment. It was intimate enough for the empathy required of the audience to be believable, and public enough to oblige the Doors to structure their performance. Still, it involved an almost excruciating intimacy. Robby:

> Jim would be on the edge of reality all the time and that's what came through in the music....I think what Morrison was trying to do and what we were trying to do in those days was reality on stage and in music. It was more like what we were really feeling than like a show or a sort of an act. We were doing what we really felt on stage.

If that pact between audience and Jim did not exist, Jim's high wire act would not work. He came to attach an almost religious value to his performances. The show was a ritual, his demands on the audience outrageous.

Clubs, the camera ecstatica, the salon, the séance. Clubs versus concerts. "We hide ourselves in the music to reveal ourselves," said Jim.

> …some of the best musical trips we ever took were in clubs. Concerts are great but it gets into a crowd phenomenon that really hasn't that much to do with music. In a club there's a different atmosphere. They can see you sweat and you can see them. And there's much less bullshit. In a concert situation, you can't really lose. You get that many people together and it doesn't really matter what you do. In a club you have to turn people on musically. If it doesn't cut it everybody knows it.... You can improvise at rehearsals, but it's kind of a dead atmosphere. There's no audience feedback. There's no tension, really, because in a club you're free to do anything. You still feel an obligation to be good, so you can't get completely loose; there are people watching. So there's this beautiful tension.

The fragility of the Doors was not surprising, given the pregnant pauses: "I like to see how long they can stand it and just when they're about to crack, I let 'em go." But the solemnity of the whole business was beginning to get to people. They laughed at Jim! When this happened in Berkeley, a wounded Jim said, "When you laugh at a performance, you're really laughing at yourselves." That Jim! What nerve! Still, what can you expect when you stop for four minutes in the middle of a song?

ﻫ

Jim habitually began Doors concerts with the triple invocation:

> Is everybody in?
> Is everybody in?
> Is everybody *in?*

Given the times, it was taken for granted that this meant

being high, but for Jim this referred only tangentially to drugs, in the sense that psychedelics themselves had become a metaphor for the one mind of Jim Steppenwolf's magic theater. Once within this charmed circle, the Cyclone began its slow climb to the first rush. Ray Manzarek:

> The Doors tried to get as far as they could, man, and take the audience with them....In the sixties ...rock 'n' roll was reality. We were up against the wall...checking out what's on the other side of the wall, of the edge. Let's get right up to the edge of madness and take a peek over.

This sort of intensity is, of course, in direct conflict with the demands of performing. For the audience, the performance is a unique experience; it happens one time, the first time, the only time. The performer must make them forget that this is something repeated night after night.

To sustain that level of obsession often means creating the conditions—by whatever means necessary. Drugs, derangement, exhaustion. If it involved an ego-fragmented Jim barking on stage, well, that's what it took.

The line between performance and life had been erased. And for this reason (and because of the strain on Jim, who kept it up on stage and off until the tour was over and beyond), the Doors never did more than five dates in a row.

The songs were structured to permit more intense exploration within the segments. John:

> There would be, like, verse and chorus and then sections for improvising instrumentally or lyrically and that's where [Jim] was free to throw anything in or do whatever he wanted.

The improvisation and raw emotion in the Doors' performance produced a volatile and unstable mix that didn't always come off. Performances were unpredictable (and not always in the way people imagined). Even in the early days, before true excess and outrage were mandatory at Doors' concerts, their performances varied wildly even from one set to the next. As when Paul Rothchild first came to see them:

> When I first heard them I wasn't knocked out at all. I saw

Of course, there was the inmate at Bellevue who wrote you every day and you had to write a letter saying please don't write anymore, my girlfriend is jealous. Bridgeport, Conn., 1968. (Photograph by Joseph Sia)

them at a first set at the Whiskey and it was a pretty bad set...the second set they were incredible.

After a year of playing with the Doors, Jim was no longer the shy, withdrawn poet who turned his back to the band while chanting his lyrics. He was now a mesmerizing performer, extending and extemporizing a multiphrenic stage presence.

The shaman whoops: Yeeeaaahhh! Robby's feedback/freakout guitar drifts, Ray hunched over his organ like the German archbishop in *Alexander Nevsky* playing the *Dies Irae* on a tiny harmonium. John's drums demarcating, clarifying, urging. Jim whirling and leaping and swinging the microphone, heaving it, the chord coiling like a cosmic serpent.

A portrait of them as a cult band by Pete Johnson in the *Los Angeles Times*:

> The Doors are a hungry-looking quartet with an interesting original sound but with what is possibly the worst stage appearance of any rock 'n' roll group in captivity. The lead singer emotes with his eyes closed, the electric pianist hunches over his instrument, as if reading mysteries from the keyboard, the guitarist drifts about the stage randomly, and the drummer seems lost in a separate world.

The Doors consider this a rave.

At lounges on the Strip—Bido Lito, Ciro's, PJ's, the Fog, the Whiskey à Go Go—the Cult of the Lizard King begins. The band attracts a fanatical species of groupie. The Doors are displacing Love as the cult group on the Strip, the hot house band.

Phil Kirby of the UCLA *Daily Brain* describes a Doors show as "Artaud Rock." Who's he been gettin' his lines from, then, eh? He describes Jim as "a gaunt, hollow Ariel from hell screaming terraced flights of poetry and music."

Jon Mendelsohn's mordant appraisal of Morrison (again in the *Los Angeles Times*) is that he is "somewhat overmannered, murky and dull...an exploration of how bored he can sound as he recites singularly simple, overly elaborate psychedelic non sequiturs and fallacies."

Taken at face value, this must have been a fairly accurate picture of Jim at the time (1966). It manages to convey the Pre-Raphaelite languor and mystery of the Doors, and would scarcely discourage potential converts to the drugged ministry of Jim Morrison. "Murky"…is that good or bad?

February 1966. The Doors' repertoire consists of some 40 songs, 25 of them originals. Jim gets out of the draft by stupefying his blood sugar, heartbeat, vision and speech. Also says he's a homosexual.

The Doors are signed by Elektra Records, up to this point essentially a folk music label. By the fall of 1966 they are recording their first album, *The Doors,* which is cut in six days. It has all of the rawness, immediacy and power of their live performances.

THE DOORS UNFOLD

The basic structure of a Doors song opens with a characteristically deceptive cocktail lounge setting ("soft and dreamy" the sheet music says). We're mildly bombed in a Gilligan's Island version of Polynesia. Drinks with the little bamboo umbrellas in them. Jim is crooning his dream-doggerel images, dragging the lyrics along with that coming-down-after-tripping lethargy, when…wait! Where are we? The room begins to hum…that loony guitar…you could be a Lithuanian at Trader Vic's. Somebody been putting something in my "Outrigger," maybe?

Suddenly, the fuel-injected Rhodes Fender bass that has been growling, idling throughout the first verse, VAR-ROOOMS to life, the purple pumping organ laden with doom and urgency, the beast who's anybody's master.

The highway is slipping past at 120 miles per hour, the landscape a blur, and the driver (Jim) has turned around to tell you something, something he's had on his mind for some time it seems. But why is he *singing?* And how did we get here?

Your only guide on this tour of hell is that Vox organ, a sort of demented Virgil. Still, in as unstable an atmosphere as this you are grateful for any anchor. Ray's electric piano is the chorus that keys the reaction, the jester commenting ironically on the mad tableaux. Jim has the soul of a sideshow freak, and this is the tune he dances to. Organ grinder, amusement park calliope, silent movie, eastern Europe, wandering gypsies, arty, bizarre Weimar decadence.

There are only a couple of songs on the first album that could be considered typically Pop, the disco thumper "I Looked at You" (their Beatles song) and "Take It as It Comes." Everything else is passing strange and gets stranger and stranger.

The first track, "Break on Through," is the Doors' first single and seems to be based loosely on "Tequila." A breathless rush, its jerky, switching syntax lurches from one idea to the next, from one state to the next, like people psychically throwing themselves against a wall of air. As a lyricist, Jim had learned from William Blake how to use extremely elementary phrases to startling effect:

> You know, the day destroys the night
> Night divides the day
>
> > "Break on Through"

The percussive quality of Jim's lyrics frequently jerks the sense along so fast so that you can't dwell on meaning. Instead, you hear an agreeable picture in 4/4 time, syllables clicking like castanets.

> She has robes and she has monkeys,
> Lazy, diamond-studded flunkies
>
> > "Love Street"

There's an edginess to Jim's lyrics right from the first album that's made all the more eerie by the source of the malaise not being identified.

> Before you slip into unconsciousness,
> I'd like to have another kiss
> Another flashing chance at bliss
>
> > "The Crystal Ship"

"Light My Fire" is the second single to be released off the first album, *The Doors,* and the song which made their reputation. A combination of sexual innuendo and drug references with apocalyptic overtones, its sleight of hand is that it manages to sound familiar and freaky at the same time.

Like most classic Doors' songs, it has an improvisational break. The long version (the one on the album) runs seven or eight minutes, most of it instrumental interlude, and is rarely played the same way twice. The way Jim sings Fy-errrr!

Jim swallowed that song whole. The long break was designed to show that the Doors were more than their lead singer. Proof, if you will, that the Doors were more than just the minions, Myrmidons to the great Achilles. But when it was decided that "this has gotta be the single," they had to go in with scissors and cut the break out.

On "Light My Fire" you can hear how Jim loved the way Elvis could tinge any ballad with sneering insolence, how he idolized Elvis as a subspecies of American religion.

> He had become obsessed about Elvis Presley and insisted
> upon silence whenever Presley's records were played on the
> radio, turning the volume up full, and sitting in front of the
> radio mesmerized.
>
> Jerry Hopkins and Danny Sugerman,
> *No One Here Gets Out Alive*

&

No wonder Buick wanted to use "Light My Fire" in a commercial. It's a jingle. As with Elvis, much of the Doors' music (and all of their image) was a kind of hallucinated kitsch. That American thing, the merchandising demon, the packaging, edge-smoothing mania—the salesman from Oshkosh or hell.

Taking that sleazy soul of the Great Consumer Continent and (with demonic ingenuity) etherealizing it. Seeking the murky soul of the beast. Hypostatized kitsch. All that! Commercials are a form of prayer, the prayers of traveling salesmen and their customers. The heart and ticking metronome of mercantilus Americanus.

Heretofore, the tendency had been to take something genuine and debase it, commercialize it. But Jim Morrison would take all that—the Popness, the production thing—and by sheer force of will make it sublime (or a close approximation).

The first album is, according to Paul Rothchild, "an aural documentary....I have never been as moved in a recording studio. I was impressed by the fact that for one of the very first times in rock 'n' roll history sheer drama had taken place on tape."

The trick was to transfer what is essentially a piece of psychological theater—ritual! transformation!—to a sound track that would evoke the absent performance. The most fragile of the performance pieces to be transposed was "The End." The dilemma: how to transmute a form of collective hypnosis into sound. It's essentially done with momentum, with shifts in the plane, the intervals, those...spaces, with Jim's enunciation, pausing between syllables.

The music generates a series of emotional states. The wash of symbols, the sitarlike guitar, the drums abruptly shifting the scene (now ominous rattles, now wagons, tumbrels to the guillotine), the organ stalking Jim's voice, the voice that has become a presence in itself, the voice of the ventriloquist.

Part of the success of this illusion comes from the interiorized images that the Doors' music projects. Compared with the stage presence of the Stones, for instance, or of Jimi Hendrix or Janis Joplin, the Doors' performances were always more psychological. No costumes, no pyrotechnics; the movie is in black and white.

The cosmic odysseys of Jimi Hendrix's urban jungle war frenzy, or of Janis's R. Crumb/Daisy Mae, were moving pictures too. But they pointed to something (however fantasy laden) that could conceivably exist in some possible world out there. The Doors imagery is internal, as if screened in a mental projection room, the Ciné Cerebellum where we watch the day's rushes. What we see is in no

"Hey, Ray, what was it that Alice Cooper used to say about Hitler being the first rock star?" The Doors taping a concert for German TV outside Frankfurt City Hall, Frankfurt, Germany, September 13, 1968. (Photograph courtesy of UPI/Bettman)

particular order, its sequence determined by mood alone. Scenes are thrown up on the screen, flash by, and are replaced by others. We are inside Jim's head, a dark cave in which rituals are performed in the light of a flickering fire, and phantasmagoric shadows are cast on the walls.

This psychological theater has its origin in a film student's perceptions, but the Doors' interpretation of it comes from television, a fragmented, imago mundi of counterpoint sequences. It's familiar in its enigmatic presentation of reality.

The ritual is finally recast in the studio, but unlike the mechanical manner of film assembly, it is traumatic re-creation. Paul Rothchild:

> I felt emotionally washed. There were four other people in the control room at the time, when the take was over and we realized the tape was still going. And all of us were audience, there was nothing left, the machines knew what to do.

ALIVE! SHE CRIED

The Doors' first bio went like this:

> On stage the Doors look like they're in their own world. The songs are spacelike and ancient. It sounds like carnival music. When it ends, there is a second of silence. Something new has come into the room.

> I've always been attracted to ideas that were about revolt against authority—when you make your peace with authority you become an authority. I like ideas about the breaking away or overthrowing of established order—I am interested in anything about revolt, disorder, chaos, especially activity that seems to have no meaning.

There probably hadn't been as strange a bio as this since the one James Dean wrote for Warner Bros. in the spring of 1954:

> A neurotic person has the necessity to express himself and my neuroticism manifests itself in the dramatic. Why do most actors act? To express the fantasies in which they have involved themselves.

The Doors' bio lists Jim's favorite vocal groups as the Beach Boys, the Kinks and Love. Jim admires Frank Sinatra,

Elvis, Jack Palance, Sarah Miles. Typically, Jim says he has no parents. They are dead. Later, Jim claims this was said to protect them. Nevertheless, like King Melchizedek, who in the Bible is said to have no mother or father, this is a cardinal fantasy of rock.

William Burroughs' Wild Boys, Peter Pan and the Lost Boys. It's what a group is: a gang, an elected family, a tribe with no history but themselves. And the Doors acknowledged neither past nor present. They existed, in rock visionary Lenny Kaye's words, "in the cruciform of Los Angeles present, a canvas in yellow and black."

☙

January 1967. Their first album, *The Doors* (with the single "Break on Through"), is released. Elektra deletes the word "high" from the single, making it an even stranger song than it already is.

Richard Goldstein in the *Village Voice* calls the album a "cogent, tense and powerful excursion." Does he mean trip? "Anyone who disputes the concept of rock literature had better listen hard and long to this song." Legitimizing rock as literature was a particular specialty of Goldstein's (at the time he was compiling his *Poetry of Rock* anthology, a volume of rock lyrics). Was rock becoming respectable?

It was "Joycean Pop," said Goldstein, but the only things that I can see Jim Morrison and Jim Joyce having in common are the monikers, prolixity and blarney. (Celts, too.)

Elektra puts the Doors on the first rock billboard, which looms above a liquor store on the Strip announcing: "THE DOORS BREAK ON THROUGH WITH AN ELECTRIFYING ALBUM." The attitude and chiaroscuro lighting of the group photo is based on early Rolling Stones album covers, but the effect is entirely different. In place of the Stones' elite bohemian arrogance and deadpan defiance, the Doors' detached heads are stacked in a row behind Ray Manzarek's solemn face, as if grimly queuing up behind their leader (a mad scientist in rimless glasses) to face some nameless fate. Their expressions are of resignation, of psychonauts who have seen too much, and their mission into the furthest regions of planet earth has not even begun.

One of the Doors' earliest gigs outside L.A. is the Fillmore West in San Francisco. They are third on the bill to the Young Rascals and the Sopwith Camel. They attend the Be-In in Golden Gate Park.

Late Spring 1967. "Light My Fire" is released as a single, and Jim and the Doors leap to fame overnight. They are immediate darlings of the underground. When their hit goes to number one by midsummer, they are also mainstream Pop/AM radio sure shots.

❧

In an age of extremes, when monsters of narcissism roam the earth declaring any number of improbable things, the Doors still manage to be electrifying. And at a time when weirdness is a virtue, the Doors are unlike anything else. There is a solemnity to their performances, a structure to their songs (however wayward they may get) that only intensifies the strangeness. There are no special effects. No one comes on stage in a flaming headdress; there are no searchlights or smoke bombs, no airborne drummer. You are not thrust into a wailing, gear-grinding Fender solo or the Owsley sawmill.

As in a *Twilight Zone* episode, it all begins so *casually* in that airport lounge. A rag-tag group of travelers whose flight has been delayed (perhaps indefinitely) is informed that their destination has been changed. Instead, their destination is to be...*change itself.* Jim saw their performances as transforming experiences, a search, "an opening of one door after another...as a snakeskin that will be shed sometime":

> Right now I'm more interested in the dark side of life, the evil thing, the moon, the nighttime. But in our music it appears to me we're seeking, striving, trying to break through to some cleaner, fresher realm.
>
> It's like a purification ritual in an alchemical sense. First you have to have the period of disorder, chaos, returning to the

Lizard King with the bends. Old Minneapolis Auditorium, Minneapolis, Minn., 1968. (Photograph by Mike Barich)

primeval disaster region. Out of that you purify the elements and find a new seed of life, which transforms all life and all matter and personality until finally, hopefully, you emerge and marry all those dualisms and opposites. Then you're not talking about good and evil anymore but something unified and pure. Our music and personalities as seen in the performance are still in a state of chaos and disorder with maybe an incipient element of purity kind of starting.

"The Doors begin where the Rolling Stones leave off," Richard Goldstein wrote in the *Village Voice*. But it was a place the Stones never intended to go. Too far. (Their motto, as expressed by Mick Jagger, has ever been, "We are always at one step removed.") This idea would have been anathema to Jim.

> The only time I really open up is on stage. I take everything really personally. I don't feel I've done a really complete thing unless we've gotten everyone in the theater on kind of a common ground. Sometimes I just stop the song and just let out a long silence, let out all the latent hostilities and uneasiness and tensions before we get everyone together.

Like his contemporaries Jimi Hendrix and Janis Joplin, Morrison was too intense to remove his flamboyant persona after his ceremonial performances were over. He had none of the ironic Brit music hall showmanship of Mick Jagger, Pete Townshend and the mates. Morrison, like Jimi and Janis, felt it would be plain phony to just take off the greasepaint and leave all that shamanistic stuff in the dressing room. That was vaudeville, show biz, the *ancien régime*. This was the ecstatic flight, the ghost dance, the song that would set you free, and these were the true believers.

The Lizard King hanging out at the bar at Barney's Beanery! The Martian Inca shopping on Carnaby Street! Pearl sashaying down Haight Street! The gods descended to earth. And just like you saw them in concert last night, man. Outtasight!

The onstage performances of these Psychedelic Avatars were more like sideshows at which aberrant behavior is exhibited. Except here, as if in some William Burroughs scenario, the audience was expected to conform to the freaks; the price of admission was, uh, like...*mutation*, man.

This change was to come about through a form of mass hypnosis, the group soul beating its synaptic wings in time to a cataleptic beat. Ray:

> You see, when the Siberian shaman gets ready to go into his trance, all the villagers get together and shake rattles and blow whistles and play whatever instruments they have to send him off. There is a constant pounding, pounding, pounding. And those sessions last for hours and hours. It was the same way with the Doors when we played in concert. The sets didn't last that long, but I think our drug experiences let us get into it much quicker. We knew the symptoms of the state, so that we could try to approximate it. It was like Jim was an electric shaman and we were the electric shaman's band, pounding away behind him. Sometimes he wouldn't feel like getting into the state but the band would keep pounding and pounding, and little by little it would take him over. God, I could send an electric shock through him with the organ. John could do it with his drumbeats. You could see every once in a while— twitch!—could hit a chord and make him twitch. And he'd be off again. Sometimes he was just incredible. Just amazing. And the audience felt it, too.

At the epicenter of the hive, the Frankenstein creature (the mutant) pulses and dances, leading the audience out of the subterranean world up through the gnarled roots to the top of the Cosmic Tree whose top touches the sky. Up on his enchanted horse through the magic of noise.

When the spirits come he begins to leap. He has left the earth! He is rising toward the clouds! At a certain moment he cries, "I am high in the air, I see Yenisei a hundred versts away!" On his way he meets other spirits, speaks, fights, implores them, and tells the audience what he sees. Then, addressing the spirit helper who is carrying him through the air, he cries: "O my little fly, rise still higher, I want to see farther!" Until he enters the second heaven, crying:

I have broken through the second ground,
I have climbed the second level.
See the ground lies in splinters

And, again imitating thunder and lightning, he proclaims:

Sagarbata! Sagarbata!
Now I have climbed two levels.

"But every genuinely shamanic trance ends in a *spectacle* unequaled in the world of daily experience," writes Mircea Eliade in *Shamanism: Archaic Techniques of Ecstasy.*

> The world in which everything seems possible, where the dead return to life and the living die only to live again, where one can disappear and reappear instantaneously, where "the laws of nature" are abolished, and a certain superhuman "freedom" is exemplified and made dazzlingly present.

Before going on stage, Jim makes a point of getting the publicist to point out the prominent rock critics in the audience, the photographers from the major magazines. In the midst of all his whirling and flailing he performs a little hypnotic psychosurgery. Tiny, preposterous, ululating phrases have been painlessly implanted by Voodoo Jim. A subsonic ululating chorus, as if chanted by two Hajjis on the bus to Shiraz: HE IS GOD WE ARE FOOLS! HE IS GOD WE ARE FOOLS!

Dazed writers stagger home. They find themselves writing these…*preposterous things!* For a moment they stare, unbelieving, at what they have just typed.

> He stepped up to the microphone, grabbed the top with his right hand and the stem with his left fingertips, and looked up so the light hit his face. The world began at that moment. There isn't another face like that in the world so beautiful, not even handsome in the ordinary way. I think it's because you can tell by looking at him that he *is* god when he offers to die on the cross for us, it's okay because he *is* Christ.

My god, did I write that, they ask? It's absurd, yes, but isn't the world, life absurd? And after, uh…ALL THIS!…man, can one seriously believe in Euclidean geome-

Like a weary Flying Dutchman he clasps the microphone stand as if it were Moses' rod, metallic crozier, the mast of his lunar pod, a wizard's technowand that could ground the lightning and put all the pieces back together. Felt Forum, Madison Square Garden, New York, N.Y., March, 1970. (Photograph by Jason Lauré/Woodfin Camp)

Jim: "We just have to hold on for a while, and one day everyone will realize ...[we're] part of our national psyche." Felt Forum, Madison Square Garden, New York, N.Y., March, 1970. (Photograph by Joseph Sia)

try, objectivity, critical distance, the integrated personality? And isn't it just possible that now, in the Age of Aquarius, an avatar has been sent to us and concealed (how divinely appropriate) as a rock star from L.A.?

❧

Meanwhile in another part of Gotham...Jim, drunk, naked, howling on his window ledge ten stories up. That beast, Demon Jim! Barking at cabs that pass him up, that have become missing words encapsulated in little mobile yellow spansules—escaped from his brain!—whole lines of lost verse tearing down 7th Avenue.

> de fus time dem kar me go a Bellevue
> was fi di dactar an de lanlord operate
> an tek de radio outa mi head...
> mi haffi sleep outa door wid de Channel One riddym box
> an de DJ fly up eena mi head
>
> Jean "Binta" Breeze, "Riddym Ravings"

Jim's performances were already reckless and possessed back in his hometown clubs. Now, out in the world, his behavior on stage took on a more frantic tension. The Doors had barely surfaced when, by the spring of that year, 1967, Jim was already "freaking out" frequently.

The reputation for anarchy, whatever-happens, anything-you-can-imagine is already so taken for granted at early Doors' concerts that Jim's frequent drunken falling into the drum kit and tumbling off the stage are thought intentional, even premeditated. Jim-nastics.

So, Jim, how do you feel now you're making it?

I can't say too much about it because we're not really making it, it's just kinda...making itself.

By midsummer "Light My Fire" is number one. Jim racing intoxicated through a Hollywood cemetery, looking for Valentino's grave.

A S u r f - B o r n D i o n y s u s

Strange Days Have Found Us.

From the very first track of the Doors' second album, *Strange Days*, the knell of doom is sounded. Like some folk-tale curse, an unnamed force has cast a pall over the land.

> Strange days have found us
> Strange days have tracked us down
> They're going to destroy our casual joys.
>
> "Strange Days"

August 1967. By the time the Doors begin recording *Strange Days*, something peculiar has happened to them. The strangeness of their first album lay in the lyrics, in the darkness of the vision, in the eruptive moodswells and psychological shifts, but in *Strange Days* everything is… *melting*. It's shot through with distortion. We're in some sort of reverberating chamber where all sonic perspective is warped.

Distortion was, of course, the *cri de cœur* of late sixties rock. For Hendrix it was an emblem of his frustration, for Janis it conveyed pain. But for Morrison distortion denoted something more impersonal and pervasive. Alienation, dread, paranoia; a prophetic apprehension, as if all the problems that would beset Morrison and the Doors in the following years were already there.

Jim turned over all the gothic metaphors of the first album one by one only to uncover even more morbid preoccupations beneath. His ongoing fixation with his own

Jim: "It's the dark side. Everyone, when he sees it, recognizes it in himself." Old Minneapolis Auditorium, Minneapolis, Minn., 1968. (Photograph by Mike Barich)

death goes back at least to the origins of the group. Scarcely had the group formed and Jim was already busy writing epitaphs. But while "this is the end, beautiful friend" was understood for what it was, youthful bravado, on *Strange Days* it's as if the unspeakable—death—has become imminent.

> Before I sink into the big sleep
> I want to hear the scream of the butterfly.
>
> "When the Music's Over"

(*The Scream of the Butterfly*, incidentally, was the title of a porno movie Jim spotted on a marquee.)

Those whose lives Morrison emulated—Rimbaud, Van Gogh, James Dean, Robert Johnson—all had the distinction of dying young, and in hindsight their sudden, violent, untimely deaths seem the only possible conclusion for their lives:

> …the mad ones, the ones who are mad to live, mad to talk, mad to be saved, desirous of everything at the same time, the ones who never yawn or say a commonplace thing, but burn, burn, burn, like fabulous yellow roman candles exploding like spiders across the stars and in the middle you see the blue center-light pop and everybody goes "Awww!"
>
> Jack Kerouac, *On the Road*

Jim's death was inevitable once he had made his pact at the crossroads. What truly possessed romantic artist would give up control over his most perfect creation, the Life of the Artist? The legend, the pocket anecdotes, the wild stories, the excesses. Would anyone ever want to open your tiny beautiful, privately printed book of verses? The walk on the wild side is proof of your passion. That you mean it. Your life demands the right ending, the perfect concluding line that will stun. Only someone who is sure that despite all the ridicule and neglect, one day that star will rise, eclipsing all the pedagogues and know-it-alls, only such a person would chance risking everything on one throw of the dice.

Jim was like the Borges character about to be executed whose last minutes of life are stretched into days to permit him to finish his epic poem. Or someone who under hypnosis sees *Gone with the Wind* replayed in an eyeblink, all in exquisite detail. The ball takes ten minutes just to fall out of the sky. That's the way it was for Jim.

The cover of *Strange Days* tells you where it's at: a strong man, a juggler, an acrobat and two midgets. The band itself appears only on a poster in the alley. We've shifted from the outside to the *inside* of Jim's head. A murky place of fits and starts, as full of anguish as any Acheron of the Ancients. It's a slightly unsettling place to be, since you know that they let you out of purgatory (eventually) but you can never get out of hell.

These songs are not being beamed to us from that sonic DMZ where much of recorded music seems to arise. This is a specific *place;* an interior with special effects. The studio! A bare padded room. Whereas the first album had been recorded close to live, *Strange Days* is very much a creature of the studio. Eight-track, state of the art for 1967. No more pingponging tracks. One of the first uses of the Moog synthesizer in rock. Whole songs are played backward, with John playing along on backward high hat. The Doors begin referring to the studio as the Fifth Door.

The most ostentatious use of their new electronic habitat is "Horse Latitudes," Jim's high school poem, to which their engineer Bruce Botnick creates a background of *musique concrète*. Hand-winding tape to resemble wind, plucking piano strings, organ tampered with electronically, dropping Coke bottles into trash cans, banging coconut shells on tile (over which Jim shouts his poem). This was an age when the transmutations of German electronic composer Karlheinz Stockhausen were seen as the *ne plus ultra*. The Beatles ("A Day in the Life"), the Stones *(Their Satanic Majesties Request)*. In 1967, everyone had a Stockhausen installment.

But not all the effects that the Doors attempt are electronic. That business of Pamela giving Jim a blow job while he's overdubbing the vocal on "You're Lost, Little Girl." In another group this would seem like wretched excess (another Led Zeppelin anecdote for you, Herr Wagner). With Jim, you know it's not *just* wretched excess. It's some striving for an absolute bond between sexuality and sound. Wretched excess of the metaphysical brand, if you like. Not surprisingly, it doesn't work.

"You're Lost, Little Girl" was the song Jim wanted Sinatra to cover. His thing about Sinatra was pretty eccentric for the sixties, a time when Frank was definitely lumped with "them." You'd never find one of Frank's records in a hippie pad. Very uncool. Only the very hip and junkies seemed to have anything good to say about him at all. But Jim is a rebel. He does his best *nouveau* Frank/Tommy Sands imitation on this track, but it's actually a bit *too* Lake Tahoe. You're back in that bar at the Morrison Hotel and, godammit, bartender, my drink hasn't been spiked.

Which brings us to "Moonlight Drive," that wacky Waikiki track, the Ur song, the song with which the Doors began. Only children, madmen, visionaries and those in love are permitted to use these primal lullaby words with impunity. Too rich for the blood of mere humans. But *an intense visitation of energy* during the year Jim spent on the beach delivered these words to him, and the moon, before his very eyes, turned into a woman's face and *I Met the Spirit of Music.* Even so…

> At last, general rule: in love, beware of the *moon* and *stars*, beware of the Venus de Milo, of lakes, guitars, rope-ladders, and of all love stories—yes, even the most beautiful in the world, were it written by Apollo himself!
>
> Charles Baudelaire, *Consoling Maxims Upon Love*

Swim, moon, climb, tide. In context (mad pingponging Hawaiian slide guitar) those McGuffey's First Reader words dissolve, their contours eroding, fusing with the notes.

Sound-conjuring vocalists like Bobby Blue Bland, Sinatra, Ray Charles and the Christmas collection album in the K Mart discount bin (various artists)—all did this to

When signals collide: Gloria Stavers' chinchilla fur (chic, androgynous), macho leathers, (hippie) Russian peasant shirt, (Native American) concho belt (not shown), Bob Dylan Spanish heels (not shown but available at all major outlets). And this is just the pedestal. The head features fashion model blow-dried hair, werewolfish face, and doomed eyes of the *poète maudit.* (Photograph courtesy of Star File/Gloria Stavers)

"Jingle Bells," but most of these guys did not read René Char for breakfast.

Paul Rothchild, speculates:

> I think what Jim wanted to be was a poet and...I don't think this is the only reason he got into it but I think that he saw rock 'n' roll, pop music as a means, a platform from which he could project his poetry.

But these impulses, the rock star and the poet, come from contradictory inclinations. Most of Jim's song lyrics have a telltale rhyme form and a more vacant, sparer, flatter quality than the poetry. The contrast is striking in the last volume of his collected verse, *The American Night*, where lyrics and poetry are printed together in the same book.

His manner of writing songs and lyrics for songs seems to bear this out.

> I heard a whole concert situation, with a band and singing and an audience, a large audience. Those first five or six songs I wrote I was just taking notes at a fantastic rock concert that was going on inside my head.

He used the beat to tack down the words, which accounts for the percussive quality of some of the songs.

> I think the music came to my mind first and then I made up the words to hang on to the melody, some kind of sound. I could hear it, and since I had no way of writing it down musically, the only way I could remember it was to try and get the words put to it. And a lot of times I would end up with just the words and couldn't remember the melody.

The wonder is that his lyrics are often so plain, that they aren't more poetic. It was sufficiently eccentric for Jim to have insisted on his being thought of as "a poet first, a rock star second." In the "mucker" philosophy of sixties rock, poetry was thought pretentious. It seemed to be everything that rock wasn't: artificial, literary, precious, academic, genteel. On the Spectrograph of Cool, poetry was as far as possible from funk. (Most rock stars wouldn't have been caught dead reading it, never mind *writing* the stuff.) Even that poet

He was a victim of millennial fever: frequent dissociative episodes involving feelings that other people, objects, or the world around him are not real, of being outside his body while intently watching himself, finding himself in a place with no idea of how he got there... Winterland, San Francisco, Calif., 1967. (Photograph by Baron Wolman)

laureate of sixties rock, Bob Dylan, when asked who his favorite poet was, answered Smokey Robinson.

So secondary to the music were the lyrics that the politically correct way of singing was to slur them as much as possible. Here's Mick Jagger on the Credo:

> I mean I don't think the lyrics are that important. I remember when I was very young, this is very serious, I read an article by Fats Domino which has really influenced me. He said, "You should never sing lyrics out very clearly."

So to have someone come along and put his lyrics on display the way Jim did was very unusual. Almost nobody, outside of folk singers and show tuners, enunciated lyrics.

Paul Simon was a big fan of the Doors and requested they be on the bill with him at one of his early concerts. But such was Jim's abhorrence of folk rock that he couldn't, despite his good old Southern manners, even bring himself to say a civil word to the man.

There's a connection somewhere between Morrison's bat about folk music and his Sinatra thing. It's the same sort of intolerance of Pollyannish pulpitry he heaped on hippie pieties. Execrated matinee prophets and salvation peddlers. Astrology? A credulous pseudoscience. Vegetarianism? For the birds.

Morrison came from another tradition, the dark path, the *poètes maudits*, the doomed geniuses. Can you see Baudelaire and Rimbaud mouthing "All You Need Is Love"? Neither could Jim. Miserable miracles! Despised long-haired panhandlers. An era when everybody was singing about peace and love, Incense & Peppermints, and there's Jeremiah Jim wailing on about night darkness, drowning, the Big Sleep, unconsciousness.

"The End" had set a precedent for the Doors. Now each album had to have a magnum opus, a long, liturgical drama. On *Strange Days* they incorporated one of the long improvisational pieces from their club days, "When the Music's Over."

The song added a new element to the already overfreighted psychomythic cargo of "The End," the petulant protest of "We want the world and we want it now!" The now, the immediate, was a further extension of the Doors' improvisational style and their insistence on "being real" on stage. If you were going to be real, nothing could be an act, rehearsed. It would have to happen in the moment. Flash, instant, jiffy, twinkling, eyeblink, nanosecond, *now!*

The sixties was the Now Generation. The word itself, *nuh-ow-uh* even has that steel guitar wah-wah dip to it. *We want the world and we want it now!* The collapsing of past and future. A demonized timeplace, the child's impatient instant gratification, the *Zein und Zeit* of existentialism, the micromandalacosm of acid, the Om of Buddhism, the zero degree of historical climate, the Eternal NOW, exasperation at 2,000 years of progress and horror. The prerecorded now.

In Bomb Culture everything had to be condensed. Cuban missile crisis. This may be the last time. *C'mon, baby, take a chance with us!* The obsession with the instant, *to kill childhood innocence in an instant.* Instant everything. *Now is blessed.* After Hiroshima, history can never repeat itself. Sex = bomb = now.

After LSD everything needed to be construed in a different perspective. Present, future, past, colliding with one another, everything converging on *us!*

THE FACE IN THE MIRROR WON'T STOP

That picture of Jim in the botanical gardens, a corona of palmetto leaves fanning into the feathered headdress of a Boraro tribesman around his head or, as if by celestial accident, the aurora of a saint.

Still, little was accidental in the way the Doors presented themselves. Their image was premeditated, packaged and slick at a time when spontaneity and rough edges were the style. They looked straight when the rage was for freakishness. Even when they presented a surrealistic picture of themselves, the effect was one of a posed still, as in that early publicity shot where Jim, naked to the waist, hand extended in mute existential gesture, is surrounded by the

Jim: "We make concerts sexual politics....The music we make goes out into the audience and interacts with them; they go home and interact with the rest of reality, then I get it back by interacting with the reality, so the whole sex thing works out to be one fine big ball of fire." Portland, Oreg., 1968. (Photograph by Douglas Kent Hall)

FOLLOWING SPREAD

The hippest club in New York at the time was Steve Paul's The Scene, a tiny blues, jazz, rock grotto in the Times Square area, New York, N.Y., June 27, 1967. (Photograph by Don Paulsen)

band, who look like his concerned caretakers. Narcissistic, glossy. Like an arty still from a movie version of *Marat/Sade*.

It's too smooth, too successful. This most famous image of Jim Morrison is so pervasive that it overrides, dominates almost everything else about him.

Before he came to New York, Morrison's voice was disembodied. To be materialized it needed a face, an image that would arise reflexively whenever you hear the Doors.

And Jim already knew what it would be. It was an image he had meditated on since adolescence. Before his first photo sessions with Joel Brodsky for *Vogue*, Jim went to see Hollywood hair wizard Jay Sebring and told him to "make me look like Alexander the Great" (what a line), showing a page torn from a history book.

Alexander, another usurper, also needed an image that would legitimize him, connect him with the occult power of the cosmos; and though it's not known what he said to his hairdresser, all portrayals of him are based on images of Helios, the sun god. In Lysippus's bust, Alexander's ringlets are made to seem extraterrestrial emanations of divine light glowing from an inexhaustible source. Louis XIV, the Sun King, had borrowed that look, as had the young Napoleon. Morrison just *took a face from the ancient gallery and walked on down the hall*.

He is first photographed by Gloria Stavers, the editor of *16* magazine. The session takes the form of a seduction ceremony and yields some self-consciously sensual and some wonderfully silly images (Jim in Gloria's full-length chinchilla coat). She sends the pix to *Vogue*.

At *Vogue* the icon is created. Bare-chested, his Indian concho belt, a single strand of beads around his neck, the combustible hair, the transfixed otherworldly gaze, the "destiny look" of national heroes and felines in general. The fixed hypnotic stare born of looking into the mirror for prolonged periods of time so often noticeable in self-portraits. And out of the mirror jumped Mojo Jim.

The singer reportedly commented on the presidential race by saying: "Four more years of mediocrity and horseshit. If he [President Nixon] does wrong, we will get him." Felt Forum, Madison Square Garden, New York, N.Y., March, 1970. (Photograph by Jason Lauré/Woodfin Camp)

Jim heliotropos, backlit by strobes to produce an image of ancient power and chemical radiance whirling around this head. It becomes his logo, his message reduced to a pictograph emitting both ambiguous and unmistakable signals.

It's the head of a Pop saint who invented and reinvented himself in a series of fabulated personae, but allowed himself to be swallowed up by his narcissistic phantom. As if the brooding, intense, charismatic Pop idol we see in these pictures had his life stolen from him and, realizing too late that he would be forever condemned to replicate these specters of himself, fell into a despondency from which he would never recover. His death further canonized him and allowed him to be manipulated by busybodies, necromancers and Hollywood.

As radio play of "Light My Fire" increases, as word of mouth spreads, as his iconic image, an Angelino Shiva, is disseminated through posters, on fan magazines, in *Time* and *Newsweek*, in *Vogue*, *Atlantic Monthly*…a new Jim Morrison—like a new Holiday Inn room—is coming into being, replicating itself somewhere in someone's head about every twenty minutes. Every twenty minutes someone somewhere in the middle of the day turns on the radio, buys a magazine, stops by a friend's house and…there it is…a new Jim! The telephonicon (sound + image) of Jim Morrison.

By the time he is a megastar at the end of the year, even people in Turkey are beginning to know who Jim Morrison is. He had made his face, as Ben Franklin said of himself, as well known as that of the moon. But Jim is getting further and further away from his self-image as a scholar-poet. That kachina doll of himself has become a little shrunken head.

Here he was, the Lord of the New Creatures, the answer to a thousand thousand prayers. But like a prophet from the wilderness made king, all he wanted was to get out. He was trapped on the other side, and could never get back.

Previously it had been the underground press, fan magazines and lefty bohemian sheets like the *Village Voice* that had swooned over the immaculate conception of Jim. Now it was the *New York Times, Newsweek, Time* and *Vogue*. All these journalists—adults!—pondering the mysteries of Morrisonia. Albert Goldman, later to become quite cynical about rock stars, back then had called Jim: "a surf-born Dionysus, a hippie Adonis." Now they were all tripping over themselves—*poveretti!*—to define the Doors. Grave middle-aged men at desks! *Newsweek* trying to get in on this, saying stuff like: "The swinging Doors open up. Chill steel, weird twangs, a howling world and forbidden fruit."

Time, like a spinster with a copy of *Lady Chatterly's Lover*, is titillated. The naughtiness of anarchy! Lifting quotes from Jim's Elektra bio, *Time* goes on to describe the music as a search that "takes the Doors past not only such familiar landmarks of youth's odyssey as alienation and sex, but into symbolic realms of the unconscious—eerie nightworlds filled with throbbing rhythms, shivery metallic tones, and unsettling images."

In that same issue of *Vogue* a professor of art history says that "Jim Morrison writes as if Edgar Allan Poe had blown back as a Hippie."

ਢ

With their place in the world fixed by the good opinion of the national press, things could not have been better for the Doors. But as fast as they had risen as the heirs apparent of rock, just as quickly things were about to come apart. The gold and silver threads of their coat of many colors were unraveling faster than even they could stitch them together. Barely a year of fame, and already it was disintegrating.

Robby Krieger muttering that what made the band such a powerful unit was the incredible psychic strength they all needed—Robby, Ray, John—just to deal with *his* excesses.

It's all connected in some horrible way. Their very success intrinsically tied to their downfall. The Doors had set such impossible goals for themselves, and the stress of performing with that intensity night after night was murderous.

It was more like a religious ritual in which something (albeit symbolic) is sacrificed. Consumed by the idea of music as pagan rite, there he was, night after night, throwing himself to the ground, humping amplifiers, clinging like Captain Ahab to the microphone, working himself into a rabid frenzy. He appeared unconscious of harm, climaxing each show as if it were his last. But unlike Pete Townshend's guitar, you couldn't always glue the pieces back together or run down to Sam Ash's and get a new one. Pieces of Osiris were being left in hotel rooms, gymnasiums, bars and airports.

This was bad enough, but it was not the Doors' only problem. (Fame is a ferocious breeder of Harpies.) Again like Alexander the Great, they had just conquered too much territory in too little time. It was becoming impossible to defend all those borders simultaneously. One satrapy was demanding hit singles; another, "art"; another, more audacious acts of revolt against authority; another, more startling poses; yet another, cultural aphorisms.

The Doors were never able to reconcile all these demands to their own satisfaction. Jim made few concessions to commerciality for its own sake, but the fact that this was unrecognized throughout much of the group's creative career produced, in retrospect, many needless problems. Feeling alternately cornered and emboldened, Jim became more and more fragmented. Meanwhile, out there somewhere, all those Jims that could never be recalled.

Digby Diehl in the *Los Angeles Times* related Jim to the polymorphous infantile sexuality espoused in Norman O. Brown's psychoarcheolinguistic classic, *Love's Body*. Jim Zeitgeist! There was nothing in the culture to which he was not seen as a touchstone. He was the *genius instanter*, the very spirit of the times. Anything you could think of, *anything at all*, he embodied it. Howard Smith in the *Village Voice*:

> There really hasn't been a major male sex symbol since James Dean died and Marlon Brando got a paunch. Dylan is more of a cerebral heart throb and the Beatles have always been too cute to be deeply sexy. Now along comes Jim

"Debbie kept saying 'I bet he isn't here' until I was ready to hit her..."
Crawdaddy! Winterland, San Francisco, Calif., December, 1967. (Photograph by Baron Wolman)

Morrison of the Doors. If my antennae are right, he could
be the biggest thing to grab the mass libido in a long time.

He was too good to be true. A teenybopper idol, an
underground hero, a Beat poet, a shaman, a dreamboat, a
rock star, a wild man who pissed on your rug, a visionary, a
stud, your drinking buddy…and on and on.

And, as if this weren't enough, there were people telling
him how he should dress, whom he should be seen with,
what caste of groupies he should hang out with. So many
hands pulling at him. Jim, honey, Gloria wants you to be
Santa Claus for the Christmas issue of *16*.…There's this
girl, Jim, you're going to flip over this chick, her name is
Nico and, you're not going to believe this, but she's more
fucked up than you are.…It's the guy from your record
company on the phone. They've got the dwarf, the clowns,
the guy on stilts, and they're down on Santa Monica pier
ready to shoot the cover.…Hey, man, you know that stuff
you were looking for, that yage shit—you know, the stuff
that Ginsberg and Burroughs were into that makes you feel
like twenty feet tall? I scored some.…

German cover girl, Nico! Lead chanteuse of the Velvet
Underground. She had once been the mistress of a famous
French ciné *divus*. An intimate of Bob Dylan and Brian
Jones. A certified decadent in Andy Warhol's *Chelsea Girls*
and Federico Fellini's *La Dolce Vita*. They are introduced
like exotic birds, like Siamese fighting fish, and retire to
Jim's room. Screams from Jim's room. They're killing each
other! Jim emerges dragging her by the hair. Perfect!

The ironical, pitiless thing was that he had been such an
enthusiastic collaborator in the manipulation of his own
image.

But there's the rub. It doesn't really matter whether you
do it to yourself or you let it happen to you. It's all the
same. But nobody told him. Unlike Elvis and Hendrix, who
allowed themselves to become victims of their managers,
Jim always seemed to be his own man. When the time
came that he felt his managers weren't doing the right thing,

"**G**et it all
out. All the little
hatreds, everything
that's boiled up inside
you. Let me have it," he
commanded. "Fuck
you," the crowd
screamed. "That's the
little word I wanted to
hear. That's the very little word," Morrison told
them. Felt Forum,
Madison Square Garden,
New York, N.Y., March,
1970. (Photograph by
Joseph Sia)

Jim: "A Doors concert is a public meeting called by us for a special kind of dramatic discussion and entertainment. When we perform, we're participating in the creation of a world, and we celebrate that creation with the audience. It becomes the sculpture of bodies in action." Felt Forum, Madison Square Garden, New York, N.Y., March, 1970. (Photograph by Joseph Sia)

out they went. He fired them—like that!—and appointed his roadie, Bill Siddons, as manager. That kind of guy. Worthy of King Solomon.

But, despite everything, the inevitable gangrene set in. Whose idea was the leather pants and concho belt? The Gloria Stavers photo session made him into a teenybopper star. Joel Brodsky made him into an international sex symbol. Yet he craved to be the dark laureate of rock, too. Not either/or, he wanted both/and. But the nature of mediated imagery is that the cruder overpowers the more subtle, the more reducible over the irreducible. The hieroglyphic transmits the message. A collapsed star, a trademark personality.

The manipulation of his image at first had been so effortless that it was just another attribute. Wasn't it he, after all, not some PR flack, who had come up with all those wonderful catchphrases like "think of us as erotic politicians"? It had been a joke. But images and slogans have a life of their own, they thrive on attention, gorge themselves on adulation and become bloated with fame.

WAITING FOR THE SUN

"The Doors, like most of their generation," Lenny Kaye pointed out in *Rock 100*, "had to decide what to do with the world once it was theirs. In a sense, the turning point had been passed with 'Light My Fire.'"

Instead of trying to heal the wound, Jim, typically, only exacerbates it. A new note of stridency and chauvinism enters the music when Morrison begins writing his most militant song, "The Unknown Soldier." Military beat, sound effects of marching feet, snare drum. This is all dramatized on stage. Jim adopts the tortured stance of a prisoner about to be executed by firing squad. A second of silence, arms held tightly by an invisible rope behind his back, his head high, his chest forward. Drum roll, John simulating a shot on the rim of his drum.

The refrain of "Five to One," another piece of antiwar artillery, meant that by 1975 there would be five younger

MR. MojoRisin'
99

people to one older person, the dividing line being over age twenty-five.

Apologists claim this song to be a parody of the naive rhetoric heard on the streets and in the underground press during the late sixties. Oddly enough, you don't get this impression from John Densmore. Or Ray:

> We all really believed it, playing at the Whiskey à Go Go, we all really believed that. Hey, man, we were gonna fuckin' take over the country, we were going to turn it around, we were going to make a perfect society.

Perhaps old slyboots hadn't clued them in. Anyway, one reason defenders of the faith claim "Five to One" is a put-on is that the conclusion is at odds with everything else in the song:

> Your ballroom days are over, baby....
> You walk across the floor with a flower in your hand
> Trying to tell me no one understands,
> Trade in your hours for a handful of dimes

The parody defense in rock 'n' roll, of course, has a long tradition: Elvis's movies, the Dylan Self-Portrait album, Stones psychedelia.

NEW HAVEN

The day after his twenty-fourth birthday, Jim is maced by a cop in a shower stall backstage before a concert at New Haven, Connecticut, while making out with a fan (or conducting a theological discussion, depending on which version you accept).

We want the world and we want it now! He spits at the audience and against the dum-dum-dum-dum-da-dada-dum rhythm of "Back Door Man" and begins telling this story:

> I want to tell you about something that happened a few minutes ago right here in New Haven. This is New Haven, isn't it? New Haven, Connecticut, United States of America? I was having a discussion about religion with a waitress, see—DUM-DE-DUM—and we wanted some

That Renaissance statue is getting larger; what had taken Elvis fifteen years Jim managed in three. Felt Forum, Madison Square Garden, New York, N.Y., March, 1970. (Photograph by Jason Lauré/Woodfin Camp)

privacy....And so we went into this shower room. We weren't doing anything, y'know. Just standing there and talking...and the this little man came in there, this little man in a little blue suit and a little blue cap....

"Whatcha doing there?"

"Nothin.'"

But he didn't go away. He stood there, and then he reached 'round behind him and he brought out this little black can of somethin'. Looked like shaving cream....

By now a phalanx of cops line the stage. They don't like this story, Jim. Tired, defeated, middle-aged men trying to make time and a half as security guards for a rock concert. And he's baiting, taunting them. DA-DA-DUM!

And then...and then, y'know what he did then, man? Sprayed the mace right in my eyes, man, RIGHT IN MY GODDAMN EYES!

Oedipus clutching his bloody sockets in agony. They—those stupid pigs, those flunkies of the tyrant Laius—have put out the eyes of King Oedipus! "The whole world hates me! The fucking world, man...nobody loves me. The whole fuckin' world hates me...." He heads into a final chorus of "Back Door Man."

The cops turn on the lights. Jim: "You want more music?" A huge roar from his subjects: YEAH! *Then turn out the lights!*

A cop walks on stage and tells him, "You're under arrest." Jim thrusts the microphone under the cop's nose. "Okay, pig, come on, say your thing, man." The cops drag Jim downstairs into the parking lot, where they kick him and punch him, charging him with "indecent and immoral exhibition, breach of the peace and resisting arrest." A minor incident, but it marks a turning point. Suddenly the Doors are on a steep Cyclone ride. Jim becomes increasingly alcoholic and violent.

In Las Vegas with Bob Gover, author of *The $100 Misunderstanding*, Jim is arrested for behaving in a drunk and disorderly manner outside the Pussy Cat à Go Go.

At singer John Davidson's house (what's he doing at John Davidson's?), the historic meeting with Janis Joplin. Being no respecter of persons, he grabs her by the hair and pulls her head into his crotch. Ends with Janis running after him, crowning him with an empty bottle of Southern Comfort. (This is one argument against that reunion in rock heaven people are always singing about.)

Bobby Neuwirth, painter, filmmaker, musician, boulevardier, *éminence grise* of rock—Dylan's Dylan—has been lured by Elektra to keep tabs on the increasingly unglued Jim, presumably on the principle that it is easier to locate two riotous maniacs than one.

At the Fillmore East in New York, despite strong protest from Bill Graham, the Doors screen their film of "The Unknown Soldier." It shows Jim tied to a post on Venice Beach and shot as movie blood gushes from his mouth.

Gene Youngblood, film critic for the Los Angeles *Free Press*: "The Beatles and Stones are for blowing your mind, the Doors are for afterward when your mind is already gone." He meant it as a compliment.

DOLDRUMS

Summer 1968. Still working on the third album, *Waiting for the Sun*. It is not going well. A long composition, "The Celebration of the Lizard," begins, gets bogged down, starts up again, falls apart, gets resurrected and is, finally, abandoned. This doesn't stop Jim from going out and having a lizard skin suit made for himself. A funny way (you too may think) to celebrate the incomparable lizard…killing a large number of them and having a suit made for yourself.

> A lizard ran out on a rock and looked up, listening no
> doubt to the sounding of the spheres.
>
> And what a dandy fellow! The right toss of the chin for you
> and swing of a tail!
>
> If men were as much men as lizards are lizards
> they'd be worth looking at.
>
> D. H. Lawrence, "The Lizard"

A short segment of the Lizard *gita* appears in "Not to Touch the Earth." The title (also the first lines, "Not to touch the earth/Not to see the sun") is straight from the table of contents of Sir James Frazer's *The Golden Bough*. A mytho-anthropologic Victorian classic of vegetation ritual and cosmic drama, it is one of Jim's bibles.

Jim, Magic Jim, logorrhea, speaking in tongues. He could write lyric poems on destinations in a bus schedule, equestrian celebrations from a racing form, time and tides. Like the schizopsychotropic girls who can read your bookshelves as titles spill into one another and jam up one against the other into frantic, voodoo verses: *Behind the Mask, Mme. Blavatsky, Psychic Pets, Green Thoughts, American Indian Picture Writing.*

But a macabre silence has fallen upon the great, sad god Dionysus. An accursed pall is cast over Mount Parnassus West. Now every song requires at least twenty takes. Most of them blown by Jim. "The Unknown Soldier" alone involves some *one hundred and thirty* starts! This isn't a new album, this is *Gone With the Wind,* John the Revelator on the Island of Patmos inscribing and wiping out those first pantocratic words, words that would echo with apocalyptic fury down 2,000 years of Western culture: "And I, Jim, saw a new heaven and a new earth...."

But those apostates among his flock—the band—are now referring to Jim's reptilian testament as "the albatross." To Jim, the Lizard is "pure drama." All his favorite themes are there: prison, insanity, dreams and death (but only two lines of the poem would be remembered), a singsongy nursery rhyme credo of narcissism:

> I AM THE LIZARD KING
> I CAN DO ANYTHING!

There they were, trapped in that studio. The very place they had so enthusiastically called "the Fifth Door." Airless, endless, a tomb with a satanic tormentor at the controls. And (like Admiral Morrison on the bridge of the *Bonny*

Pamela
Courson and Jim in Muir
Woods outside of San
Francisco, Calif., 1967.
Jim called her "his cos-
mic mate." She said
"I'm Jim's creation."
They met in 1966 and
were inseparable (in
their fashion) until the
bitter end. (Photograph
© 1967 Bobby Klein,
courtesy FAHEY/KLEIN
Gallery, Los Angeles)

FACING PAGE
Witnesses
said Morrison made
obscene gestures with a
scarf and threw it to
the crowd of screaming
youngsters. Felt Forum,
Madison Square
Garden, New York, N.Y.,
March, 1970. (Photo-
graph by Joseph Sia)

Dick) he's telling them: "Let's try it one more time, guys… we're almost there." Another take. Who do I have to fuck to get out of this movie? On the intercom a horrible voice, a voice from hell, reminds the Lizard King of his oath. It's Paul. Paul, uh…Rumpelstiltskin! And he's *saying it again*: You must spin more gold! You may not leave until you have produced another RIAA-certified million-selling album.

And still there was nothing. No words, no rhymes, just the grisly echoing wet-brain phrases that would not adhere, would not form into verses. Where were those terrible yoked horses of song, iambic pentameters that once thundered over the tundra and turned miraculously into couplets? Those bicameral voices that had insinuated all manner of fantastic things to him since childhood had vanished. The Castilian font…*dried up!* The muse had deserted him; he could no longer charm a sestina, a villanelle, a mere quatrain out of her. And those sullen Myrmidons of yours: Ray, Robby and John—staring, whispering, hand-wringing, gestures of exasperation. Don't they know, Magic Jim, that your three wishes are up?

But wait, Jim, think back, baby. What about those old journals from the days when, carefree, you lived on that rooftop in Venice, man? Jim, the Dharma Bum. And inspiration flowed out of you. That dynamite stuff about TV antennas and Hopi creation myths….You *burned* them? *All* of them? Jim, how could you? Two thousand mikes of Owsley Sunshine? Christ, that would do it! Say, maybe we could get you hypnotized (Jim wants sodium pentathol) and then…maybe you could…*rewrite* those pages and then we could finish this fucking album and the studio police would let us go home.

Wait! Something's coming through. The psychotemporal parasites are humming in Mad Jim's head and singing each to each. Holding both hands to his head over the headphones, he does a slight dance and softly shouts "Hello, I love you, won't you tell me your name?" He repeats it, nervously.

The Fisher King has broken the spell. The clouds open, and the sharp Andalusian light that precedes rain, crucifixions and revolutions floods the brain. The sun! Perhaps it had been bad luck to call the album, in at least one of its incarnations, *Waiting for the Sun*.

> To shine—
> and the hell with everything else!
> That's my motto—
> and the sun's!
>
> Vladimir Mayakovky, "An Extraordinary Adventure"

That sound we hear on "My Wild Love," is it jubilation, the tintabulation of happy release—everybody clapping hands, feet stamping in unison?

❧

Joan Didion attends one of the *Waiting for the Sun* sessions with her husband, John Gregory Dunne, who wants Jim and his buddy Tom Baker (R.I.P.) to play charismatic junkies in the movie Dunne's producing, *Panic in Needle Park*. They come to see him because he has become a monument in L.A., like Tolstoy at Yasnaya Polyana or Ezra Pound in Rapallo, a living relic who is a part of every civilized tourist's itinerary.

Bobby Neuwirth had been hired by the band to make a 16mm black-and-white documentary, *Not to Touch the Earth*, the prototype for future rock promotion videos. Not that tapes or kinescopes of rock groups hadn't been made before, but these were usually filmed performances from shows like *Ready, Steady, Go!* rather than videos specifically made for rock TV. Neuwirth:

> The idea was the Doors would never have to do the Dick Clark show or some of the other shows. They would just send over the latest films. That way nobody'd have to move any amps and nobody'd [Jim] have to be sober.

ENSENADA

The odd thing (or was it?) is that just at that moment when the lyrics were shriveling up Jim was getting seriously back into his poetry. Unlike almost anything else he did, he treated his poems with a tidy reverence, typing and retyping them neatly on sheaves of foolscap.

Pamela Courson arranges a meeting with Beat liturgical poet Michael McClure. The Beats were living saints to Jim. Beats were these *essential* guys, the real thing. That's what Beat meant: beaten down, furtive, reductio ad Bardo, shaved by Occam's razor. Too beat to fake it. And here was Michael McClure, to some the best of the Bardo bards, writer of sexual-industrial mantras, enigmatic slang, Minotaur-at-the-end-of-your-mind verse. He who had hung out with Kerouac ("you could hear his cranium creak as he crossed the room") and Ginsberg, and could with one *cool gesture* beckon him in from the Pop maelstrom into that sanctum sanctorum of philosopher-poets and wry boozy mystics railing against fate, wenches and landlords!

The first meeting was a disaster. McClure, probably imagining the verse Pamela had sent him to be driveling star babble, hadn't got around to actually reading any of it. (There was a feeling, as with Kerouac, that anybody who was that popular, that good-looking even, couldn't be any good.)

When Jim shows up at a McClure performance in one of his characteristic bouts of shyness, he gets falling-down drunk. Speechless as one of McClure's growling Buddhist beasts:

> Blue Black Winged Space Rainbow GRAHHR
> Black Winged GRAHHR Toes Kiss
> Pink Leather GRAHHR Blue Rainbow
> Vapor GRAHHR Vapor GRAHHR
> Hahr Rainbow Space Black Yahr
> GRAH! GRAH!
> White Mount Toes Kiss
> Toes Kiss Star.
>
> Michael McClure, "Grahr Mantra"

STAR CURSE

Jim was becoming weary of rock stardom, but it wasn't going to be so easy to check out of Hotel California. It was

as if you had once been an overweight king of Egypt and then wanted to be something else…It could never be. If, say, you became a brilliant exegete of Sanskrit poetry, a cosmologist, an inventor of a revolutionary new barbecue sauce …still, you'd always be known as "Fatty Farouk, *ex-King of Egypt,* now King of the Barbecue Pit." It was the same with Jim.

Even the Doors, the band that Jim and Ray had first conceived of as an almost Symbolist rock group—Art Rock!—were now just another unit out there trying to climb back up the grubby rungs of *Billboard* and *Cashbox* along with Tommy James and the Shondelles. Whatever you said you were, whatever you tried to do, you always ended up as… *this*! Number 16 with a bullet. Another group-eat-group band on Cousin Brucie's triple-play countdown. The Rimbaud of rock had become a "sex idol," another pin-up from Personality Posters.

What Jim and Ray had started out to do was to create this band that would—don't laugh—transcend rock. The Doors would be "an intelligent, volatile fusion of theater, poetry, and well-executed exploratory music." A deadly, pretentious idea perhaps. Anyway, once the Crystal Ship began rolling, all this fuddy-duddy stuff about higher aspirations got eaten alive by Demon Rock.

That group soul, the Doors, had taken on a life of its own. It was now a separate entity, out of control and careening down the American airwave highway like a sleek new Shelby GT-500 Coba. Call it what you will, it's a Pop song now, boy. It's out there, and what's out there partaketh of out there. The Doors are just another rack job, another unit for West Coast promo men to hustle. Now at the unbelievably low, low price of $3.99! Merchandise, baby!

In an attempt to show his contempt for their fawning adulation, Jim had taken to spitting at his audiences. All those radiant, intoxicated faces in the front row. They loved it! Blessed saliva of the gods, *his* bodily fluids drenching them, the soma of the Thunder God. Jim would get shitfaced drunk and hector them, but this only excited them more. He cares! The sex idol, the Lizard King.

Jim fueled the fire almost without thinking about it. Limits were to be crashed, authority and decorum were to be trampled, ridiculed. Everything in excess!

> I think the highest and lowest points are the important ones. All points in between are, well, in between. I want freedom to try everything—I guess to experience everything at least once.

Mojo!

TURBULENCE

Two things were happening simultaneously: the turbulence created by Jim's fucking up (the Doors' descent), and the Doors' steady rise to fame. Although they say Jim is "ravaging that voice he had with drink," he is voted Vocalist of the Year in the *Village Voice* (1968 poll). Also, the Doors are Best Newcomer of the Year (for 1967) and Ray Manzarek is Best Musician of the Year (after Eric Clapton and Ravi Shankar). The Doors are second only to *Sergeant Pepper*. A seven-page spread in *Life* makes a case for their literacy and validity.

Note of Doom #2. Jim wants out of the band. Tribal voting: he only has one vote in four, but he can't be outvoted. The band is rolling, why quit now? Six more months, Ray pleads.

July 5, 1968. Extravaganza at the Hollywood Bowl. Jim has preconcert dinner with Mick Jagger. The Doors are now being sold as "America's Rolling Stones." Picture this: It's the Hollywood Bowl, the Doors are being filmed, and—here you have to take your hat off to Jim—he drops acid backstage!

His name has become a mantra: "Morrison! Mor-ri-son! More-is-sun." An invitation to riot. The Mexican peon shirt. The writhing on the floor, the emblematic James-Dean-at-the-opening-of-*Rebel-Without-a-Cause* fetal position. The fatalistic poseurs. Based on Manet's *Dead Bullfighter*.

The album originally called *American Nights*, then renamed *The Celebration of the Lizard* (Jim wanted the cover in imitation lizard skin), and finally called *Waiting for the Sun* is at the top of the charts. (The title song gets left off.)

A complete version of "The Celebration of the Lizard" would ultimately appear on the Doors' performance album, *Absolutely Live*. For Jim a lizard was never just a lizard.

> We must not forget that the lizard and the snake are identi-
> fied with the unconscious and with the forces of evil. There's
> something deep in human memory that responds strongly to
> snakes. Even if you've never seen one. I think that a snake
> just embodies everything we fear...["The Celebration of the
> Lizard" is] kind of an invitation to dark forces.

The malign chthonic powers of the reptile, however, are not to be confused with his persona, the Lizard King:

> It's all done tongue-in-cheek. I don't think people realize
> that. It's not to be taken seriously. It's like if you play a vil-
> lain in a western it doesn't mean that's you. That's just an
> aspect that you keep for the show, I don't really take that
> seriously. That's supposed to be ironic.

The single, "Hello, I Love You" tops the singles charts.

Riot # 2. Phoenix, Arizona. "NEAR-RIOT ERUPTS AT COLISEUM" headlines the *Phoenix Gazette*.

> Last night the State Fair being held at the Coliseum erupted
> into a war between kids and cops. Blame it on the Doors,
> possibly the most controversial group in the world. Lead
> singer Jim Morrison appeared in shabby clothes and
> behaved belligerently. The crowd ate up Morrison's antics
> which included hurling objects from the stage to the audi-
> ence, cussing, and making rude gestures.

The Doors acquire cachet with the underground. Jim is in *Vogue* again.

EURO + POETRY #2

October 1968. Granada TV presents a documentary, *The Doors Are Open*. It juxtaposes concert footage of the Doors at London's Roundhouse with footage of the Democratic

FOLLOWING SPREAD
1967.
Now they're really pulling the image together. The Doors' second group publicity photo is a quantum leap from the Bronson Caves session the year before. The chiaroscuro from early Stones album covers, the cool from *nouvelle vague* movies and just a tiny tornado starting to brew in Jim's right eye. (Photograph courtesy of UPI/Bettman)

Convention in Chicago and demonstrations at the American Embassy in London.

In Amsterdam, Jim is offered a huge chunk of hashish and, as is his custom, swallows the whole thing. Collapses on stage and is hospitalized.

Producer Elliott Kastner wants him to play Billy the Kid in a movie adaption of Michael McClure's *The Beard*. Boozy pub crawling with McClure and the obligatory visit to the Lake District where Wordsworth, Coleridge, Southey and Lamb cavorted.

Like everyone else who'd ever hung out with Magic Jim (and been pleased to drink his booze and eat expensive trays of stuff on doilies sent up from room service), maybe McClure had hoped he wasn't going to be made to read this stuff. Or worse, subjected to a reading. Those carefully typed, crisp pages on 60-pound laid Baseldon Bond paper. And Jim sitting there, waiting for you to finish. Endless, awkward moments and you're thinking, God! What if this is like, say, Red Skelton's paintings?

As if Louis XIV woke up one morning and thought he was Racine. "Call in Cardinal Richelieu. I want to try out some pentameters on him." Well, what do you do? Or if Stalin (didn't he write poetry, too?) or Hitler asked you in. The *Führer* wants your candid opinion on this watercolor he's just dashed off.

Then you open up one of the notebooks and, uh, what is this? The world is on fire! Ghosts in cars! The barking of ancient dogs! Taxis from Africa!

Say, this is the real thing. The grand old American bardic tradition. What a relief!

McClure encourages Jim to put out his poems in a privately printed edition, "like Shelley, man."

Pamela Courson is his editor ("she goes through it and takes out all the *fucks* and *shits*"). McClure: "Mark Twain's wife did that, too." He tells Jim:

> Do you know that William Carlos Williams poem "The Red Wheelbarrow"? It's one of the great objectivist poems

and relates to the Ensenada poem of yours. It reminds me of "Red Wheelbarrow" in its concreteness and length... although it's impressionistic in technique it moves through space like film does, like a movie.

Let's go to the foliotape. *The American Night*, volume two, of his posthumously collected poems. Out of the first four stanzas slither hallucinatory images (black neon, Italian silk skin, flaming hair, india ink, desert seas) that, in turn, flash into yet other pictures, catch on fire and are themselves replaced. The narration is less like that of film than of someone receiving (about every twenty seconds) a very odd postcard from Max Ernst.

No idea what's going on here but we like it. We expect nothing less of High Modernism. But, dear sir, what on earth is the meaning of the following? *Jail is a pussy coil, dry as meat, dog-faced, clever.* Oh nevermind. Next, we're a dog leaping a wall, talking that talk, barking that Dada Quest-for-Fire Cromagnonspeak ("mate follows leap to suffer/String-throat, hollow, madness cry"). Honi soit qui Malibu, indeed.

The maddening thing in the end about Morrison's poetry is what is maddening about the Doors. It's all so lopsided. As soon as you come to the conclusion that what's going on is sheer inspired genius, you come upon something that's, well, not.

ESCALATION

Feast of Friends, the movie they've "spent a fortune on," is finally finished, although the look of it is deliberately *un*-finished. It has the rough-cut quality of Dylan's adrenaline-spliced documentary, *Eat the Document*.

There are some wonderful effects, the ectoplasmic double exposures of Jim's singing head and thrashing body superimposed on performance shots. Those overexposed images forming furious specters that leap out of the audience—do I spy Mojo Jim?—wrap around Jim and the band in a narcissistic embrace.

But the most salient feature of the film is...pandemonium, riots! While Jim is writhing on stage in mock agony,

FOLLOWING SPREAD

Ray looks on with horror-tinged bonhomie as the human firecracker lights his fuse. Frankfurt City Hall, Frankfurt, Germany, September 13, 1968. (Photograph courtesy of UPI/Bettman)

not-so-mock situations are erupting everywhere. Wild-eyed fans climbing over one another to get onto the stage. The police heaving them back, like demons from a medieval painting throwing the damned back into the pit. Jim:

> The first time I saw the film I was taken aback because being on stage and one of the central figures of the film, I only saw it from my point of view. Then, to see a series of events I thought I had some control over…to see it as it actually was…I realized I was only a puppet of a lot of forces I only vaguely understood. It was kind of shocking.

By now audiences wanted nothing less than Armageddon from a Doors concert, apocalypse now. Uproar! Tumult! Revolution! The Doors (read Jim) were guaranteed to do things you didn't get from other groups. Stoned, stumbling off the stage, drunk, screaming his way through forgotten verses, humping amps. A freak show. Direct experience! Total reality!

In all this some things would, naturally, have to fall by the way. The music…lyrics…in short, almost everything the group originally espoused. It was now the Riot & Transcendence Company. Living theater. On stage it was the end of the night, the end of time.

And the audiences' expectations are becoming impossible to satisfy. This, combined with Jim's quest for the absolute and wretched excess, is steadily upping the ante. What would that crazy Jim do next? Hey, the last audience had a riot in Drive-thruville, where's ours?

At the early concerts it had been easy to amaze. Now they want *everything you can possibly imagine!* Sometimes Jim felt ecstatic; just as often he felt unworthy of all this unwarranted adulation, this mindless idolatry. He became more and more frantic about what to do about it.

The situation is only aggravated by the Doors' general unwillingness to play auditoriums that hold fewer than 10,000 people. The problem has become exponential. A 10,000-seat auditorium is not just a very large club; it's a completely other kind of space, an arena, more like a circus.

Jim: "I did try and create something a few times just because I'd always heard about riots at concerts and I mean I thought we ought to have a riot.... You know what, soon it got to the point where people didn't think it was a successful concert unless everybody jumped up and ran around a bit." Felt Forum, Madison Square Garden, New York, N.Y., March, 1970. (Photograph by Joseph Sia)

Unlike the music-hall-based English groups who could (and did) exaggerate their already stylized acts into hippo-drome pantomimes, the subtlety that was at the heart of the Doors' psychological theater was lost in these vast spaces. Robby:

> Sometimes he would fall on the ground and writhe around like a snake. I knew Jim didn't really mean all that stuff, but I knew he was into it, too, and I knew he had to push himself to do more and more as the crowds got bigger. I felt sorry for him.

Jim's chronic cry became: "What do you want? *What?*"

But now wild behavior was not just what was expected; it had become the directive, the star imperative.

At the Doors' first hometown appearance since the Hollywood Bowl, the audience begins throwing handfuls of sparklers at the stage. Growling like a baited bear, Jim snarls back: "Hey, man, cut that shit out. Cut that fucking shit out." The populace murmurs against him. "Shut your holes!" Noises, shouts, catcalls.

> What are you doing here? Why did you come tonight? Waal, man, we came to play music all night, but that's not...what you really want, is it? You want something else, something *more*, something greater than you've ever seen before, right?

The fans howl back. They think it's a come on! "Waal, fuck you, we came to play music." And into "The Celebration of the Lizard."

January 1969. The Doors are "the American Beatles," the biggest American group. They are making $40,000 a night. In *Saturday Review,* Ellen Sander calls Jim a "Mickey Mouse de Sade." (Even when putting him down, journalists can't lay off the superlatives.)

Miami, Paris, Death and Resurrection

Prelude to Doom!

Morrison had been a true believer in Artaud's Theater of Cruelty as far back as his days at Florida State. Now, the living embodiment of the theater of confrontation was coming to Los Angeles—the Living Theater. He buys a block of tickets for every performance.

February 28, 1969. Jim goes to see the Living Theater's *Paradise Now!* The Living Theater was everything you could possibly want, and they wanted just as many impossible things before breakfast as Jim did. They were truth seekers, hypnologists, freedom fighters, millennial warriors, Utopians, priests of Thespis. And they were against just about as many things as Jim was against, too. Against the establishment, repression, national borders, drug laws, propriety, antinudity ordinances. Whaddya got?

Meanwhile, Jim is drinking heavily and eating little white pills. He is blown away by the performance, but comes out of it with a terrible revelation about himself and the Doors. Hadn't they betrayed their role as artists, sacrificed their mess of potage, and become mere...*entertainers?*

Hadn't Morrison himself written in his "Notes on Film" *(The Lords & The New Creatures)* that once upon a time the shaman, made delirious by drugs, dancing and chance, had mediated between the human and the spirit world, through his "professional hysterics."

But the gods no longer speak with mortals. We are in a fallen world, segregated into actor and spectator, star and fan. Idolmakers who both revere and punish their idols.

Jim's grave in the Père Lachaise cemetery in Paris is a shrine where fantasies are consecrated in a palimpsest of graffiti. Paris, France. (Photograph by Louis De Carlo)

Dominican Republic
Elaine
Filipo
1/8/90
KUNJAR
ROAD HOUSE
Bendix
OUTLIVE DEATH!
NICO
DIDIER
JIM MORRISON
BARRY
CHRIS
VILLASANTA
E' PRESENTE
JACK DANIEL'S

He had a way of looking out of the frame as if an unseen hoard of demons were approaching far off. Winterland, San Francisco, December, 1967. (Photograph by Baron Wolman)

Few performers could shut their eyes with such dramatic emphasis as Jim. Winterland, San Francisco, Calif., December, 1967. (Photograph by Baron Wolman)

Jim in the process of turning himself inside out (the Möbius hug), Winterland, San Francisco, Calif., December, 1967. (Photograph by Baron Wolman)

Jim's performances are a fluent history of signifying postures from the Renaissance symmetry to Romantic agony. Winterland, San Francisco, Calif., December, 1967. (Photograph by Baron Wolman)

We have metamorphosized from a mad body dancing on hillsides to a pair of eyes staring in the dark.

Paradise Now! propelled Morrison to return with messianic zeal to the true faith with which the Doors had begun. No more "performances." From now on it would be nothing less than Complete Being every night. Total Reality on stage. *Entelecheia!*

MR. MIAMI MOUTH

Those two words—*paradise* and *now!* (with that terrible inquisitorial exclamation point)—pursue Jim relentlessly. Stalking him through that drunken stopover in New Orleans, they provoke a fight with Pamela and get on a plane with him to the big homecoming concert in Florida (they'd already made him miss two flights). Talismanic words.

Jim has no sentimental feelings whatsoever about going back to Florida. "Went to school down here," he tells the audience (cheers), "but then I got smart and moved to a *beautiful* state called California." How to win friends.

March 1, 1969. The Dinner Key Auditorium in Miami, Florida. Some 17,000 kids packed into a seaplane hangar on a steamy Southern night, a raging, overamped Morrison, boiling with a witch's brew of pentecostal zeal and self-loathing. Twenty minutes into the set and Jim has yet to appear. Like the last fever-ridden conquistadors straggling through an infested rain forest behind a fanatical and demented Pizarro, the Doors were prepared for anything Jim might have up his sleeve. Ray:

> John, Robby, and I didn't know what Jim would do. We'd follow him into the jaws of the hellhound itself, if we had to, 'cause this is Jim, this is our man, this is our main man—the poet.

He staggers onto the stage, slurring, rowdy, eruptive.

> I'm not talking about revolution. I'm talking about having a good time...We're gonna lie down in the sand and rub our toes in the ocean...LOUDER, *c'mon* band!...Hey, listen, I'm lonely. I need some love. Ain't *anybody* gonna love my

Jim: "Our music is like someone not quite at home, not quite relaxed. Aware of a lot of things, but not quite sure." Portland, Oreg., 1968. (Photograph by Douglas Kent Hall)

ass? Nobody gonna come up here and love me, huh? All right for you, baby. I'll get somebody else....

It's Happy Hour at the Morrison Hotel Saloon, and Jim is just the drunk on the next barstool (your Uncle Jack), insulting and apologizing, confiding, threatening, self-pitying.

> Lettin' people push you around. How long do you think it's gonna last? Maybe you love it, maybe you love gettin' your face stuck in the shit....You're just a bunch of slaves! You're ballroom days are over, baby, night is drawing near....

He puts his thumbs into the tops of his leather pants, he's playing with the buckle. Roadie Vic Treanor runs out on stage and grabs the belt from the back, pulling it tight so Jim won't be able to undo it. But that Mojo takes down his pants anyway and (what a joker) he's wearing this huge pair of flowered boxer shorts underneath. He'd planned it!

And just then an old acquaintance comes up to the stage with a lamb, and hands it to Jim. The image is fiendish, Black Bart in his Mephistophelian beard and shades, with the leather hat with the skull and crossbones on it. That white lamb, the very epitome of innocence, of the victim about to be sacrificed to the Demon. And Jim knows just what to say: "I'd fuck her, y'know," he tells the audience, "but she's too young."

Over and over, Preacher Jim, all dressed in black, exhorts his flock: "There are no limits! There are no rules!"

In time, things would change, but today—now!—he could see the future. A foreign country ("people do things differently there") just beyond most people's heads. The thinnest of membranes separates us from it. Morrison would rip it open, and the future would come pouring out. If only he could make everybody see it. The homeless, lost, tormented, the fellaheen, the fallen bureaucrats, the people in the balcony. And it was right there, vibrating just beyond that...screen. In an instant, everything would be set right. All it would take was that first act and that kiss of violence.

> Hey, listen, I used to think the whole thing was a big joke.

I thought it was somethin' to laugh about, and then the last couple of nights I met some people who were doin' somethin'. They're tryin' to change the world, and I WANNA GET ON THAT TRIP! I wanna change the world.

For an hour Jim coaxes the audiences to come up onto the rickety stage. To testify, to dance. "We're not leaving until we get our rocks off!" Eventually there are over a hundred people on stage and it is wobbling wildly. It's about to collapse. But this is so irrelevant, wherefore wouldst thou concern thyself with such matters as personal safety, O my brothers, at this the eleventh hour? And just then one of the security men flips Jim off the stage and into the audience.

What timing! Jim picks himself up like a cartoon character and forms a human snake, dancing through the auditorium, up into the balcony, entreating his followers to cast off their clothes. Which they do. Piles of panties, bras, shirts up to four feet high are later collected.

The following day, the *Miami Herald* is claiming Jim Morrison threw three policemen off the stage. And suddenly all the parents of all those kids who came home like little savages with no clothes on start getting on the hooter. Finally, five days later, Jim is charged with three misdemeanors (indecent exposure, open profanity and drunkenness) and one felony that claims that Jim "did lewdly and lasciviously expose his penis, place hands upon his penis, shake it, and further the said defendant did simulate masturbation upon himself and oral copulation upon another."

If convicted of all charges, Jim stands to get 7 years and 150 days in the notorious Raiford Prison. The FBI also charges him with unlawful flight, despite the fact that the complaint is issued five days after he has left Miami. On April 4, Jim surrenders to the FBI and is released on $50,000 bond. In the background, banshees like Anita Bryant are wailing with self-righteousness. Jackie Gleason, Pat Boone—even Nixon wants to get in on it. Their most obscene act—a Rally for Decency.

FOLLOWING SPREAD

The Doors, 1966. Bronson Caves, Hollywood, Calif., was a favorite place for groups to have their glossies shot. (Photograph © 1967 Bobby Klein, courtesy FAHEY/KLEIN Gallery, Los Angeles)

Miami was to have been the first stop of the Doors' long-awaited First Real Tour. It would instead be the last stop, and the beginning of the end. Rather than making the national breakthrough tour they had been anticipating, the Doors end up on vacation in Jamaica.

Jim has rented a huge plantation house, and spends several days there with no one but himself, a houseful of servants and some very strong Jamaican ganga. It's a scene from Buñuel. Lord Jim by himself in this huge colonial house, high as a kite, with the servants just standing around. Land of magic spells and curses. The plantation owner's wayward son alone in that spooky, wind-creaking house filled with Yoruba spirits. Perhaps the servant has put a powerful potion in his Malaga wine.

そ

The trial takes place in the fall. Morrison is ultimately cleared of all but the lesser charges, but nevertheless gets the max: six months in jail, a $5,000 fine. He is released on bail.

Ray has said that—since Jim never actually exposed himself—what happened was a "mass hallucination, a Miami version of the vision of Lourdes…people saw snakes instead of the Virgin Mary, but there were no snakes."

If so, this act of illusion was Jim's triumph. It was an event he had been rehearsing all his life. The odd thing about the Miami Incident is that in the end he was convicted for something he *might have done*. That a number of people became convinced they did see "it" in spite of a mass of cumulative evidence to the contrary shows how indelible his image had become, how mesmerizing his conjuring power was.

He had made them see snakes, had pulled them out of thin air the way a shaman summons totemic birds. (Then again, he may also have pulled them out of his pants.) When Pamela asks him if he did it, Jim says, "I just wanted to see what it looked like in the spotlight."

And what sorcery! What demonic ingenuity! To involve all these fantastically straight people in his own martyrdom.

Aldermen, vice squad time servers, housewives, county court file clerks, orange juice hucksters, aging TV comics— what a cast!—and they're all in this huge production that unbeknownst to them has been scripted and directed by (and is, of course, starring) Jim Morrison! He's got policemen, judges, even the goddamn FBI involved. What a great scene, man, when they make the movie of my life.

> I see myself before an enraged mob, in front of a firing squad, weeping uncontrollably about my fate (something *they* wouldn't understand) and I forgive them! Just like Joan of Arc! "Priests, professors, big shots, listen to me, you're making a big mistake taking me to court over this thing. I have never been one of you. Barely civilized, I come from a race that sang under torture. Your laws confuse me, can't you see I have no moral sense whatever, I am a savage and this is all a terrible misunderstanding...."
>
> Arthur Rimbaud, *A Season in Hell*

Miami served another purpose, too, although perhaps more dramatically than Jim had imagined. The powers that be would finally have to see him for what he was, le nouveau Jim. He'd changed, or hadn't they noticed? After Miami, pictures of Jesus Christ in overalls were plastered all over the place, and yet everyone—his record company, the audiences, even those crusaders through the fires of hell, the Doors—refused to see it.

"I tried to reduce the myth to absurdity," Jim said of the whole brouhaha. "Now let's see Buick use 'Light My Fire.'"

But Miami is by no means the end of the Doors' woes. On the contrary, now *every* performance seems to present new threats. There are more indecency charges, more drunk-and-disorderly incidents, a claim by two airline stewardesses that they've been raped. Every small-town sheriff and mayor running for office is out to make a quick name for himself as a champion of decency. They smell blood. Officers of the peace now show up at concerts with blank warrants made out in the name of each of the Doors. Promoters start putting in a "fuck" clause in their concert contracts. The Doors suspect their limo drivers are narcs.

As a precaution, the band begins taking their own cops with them to avoid confrontations with the local variety. They hire six detectives from the Sullivan Detective Agency of Philadelphia to serve as security guards at their concerts.

Robby's nightmare:

> Jim called me last night at 4:00 A.M. You know what he said? I was half asleep, mind you, and he said, "This is god calling and we've decided to kick you right out of the universe!"

This was the Doors' problem in a nutshell. Jim was the *roi soleil*, the center of the Doors' universe. They must have realized early on that without him their star would collapse. Without Jim they were nothing but…white dwarfs. And their sun was burning out.

The Doors were in a holding pattern somewhere out over the Pacific in this huge jumbo jet, and the pilot was getting extremely unpredictable. It was ironic that the group who insisted on change and metamorphosis from its audiences had itself got stuck in such a rut. In a way, the Doors had become static, Ptolemaic.

Morrison himself was not unaware of this dilemma. As he said to Fred Myrow, Leonard Bernstein's assistant: "If I don't find a new way to develop within a year I'll be good for nothing but nostalgia." A fate he regarded with horror. A sixties oldies show in Las Vegas with Jim stuffed into those leather pants, still falling down drunk, lurching off the stage. Promoters in the future would have insisted on this aspect of Jim's performance, even if he had been in AA.

&

Waiting for the Sun was a classic example of third album drought. Bands starting out usually have enough material for their first two albums, but by the time they get to the third one the cupboard is bare. There's no time; nonstop touring, shopping, drugs, etc. All this compounded by the lack of new experiences (beyond room service, groupies and limo drivers).

And things only got worse with the fourth album, *Soft*

Parade. Many people who bought it were not sure what they were listening to. The whole of side one was just like…Uncle Jack! And the old lounge lizard now had the whole Mike Douglas Orchestra behind him. Strings from the Los Angeles Philharmonic and horn-section studio musicians further diluted the once primal Doors sound. It was what roadie Vic Treanor called the LaCienega Symphony sound.

On the other hand, *Morrison Hotel* (the fifth album) is a considerable improvement over the previous two. Bluesy, funky, no more horns and strings. But the mood isn't exactly mellow. (There are frequent flareups in the studio between Robby and Jim.) The very first song they ever recorded, "Indian Summer," is dusted off and included. ("The Spy" from this album was used in the soundtrack of Brian DePalma's *Body Double*.)

The album gets good reviews generally. "Returning to the tight fury of early Doors' music/burning with funk and guts and earth energy" type of thing. It is around this time that Jim, in keeping with his dedication to the sleazy side of life, checks in to the seedy Alta-Cienega Motel on the Strip.

As sessions for their final album—*L.A. Woman*—start up, Paul Rothchild decides to walk: "I'm not interested anymore, guys. That one song about the killer on the road sounds like cocktail jazz to me. You should produce it yourselves, probably do fine."

They do. With engineer Bruce Botnick, they move all the equipment over to 8512 Santa Monica Boulevard, put the recording board upstairs in Bill Siddons' office and the console on his desk. They come in at night, move the furniture, put blankets on the walls, use the office as the control room.

Italian film director Michelangelo Antonioni comes to one of the sessions of *L.A. Woman* and asks Jim to write music for his new film *Zabriskie Point*. Jim writes the song "L'America." A synthetic history of the Americas filled with pirate imagery.

❧

FOLLOWING SPREAD

Either modeling a statue by Donatello or lost in the blooze (or both). Tony Glover (second from right) sits in on harmonica. Old Minneapolis Auditorium, Minneapolis, Minn., 1968. (Photograph by Mike Barich)

There is serious talk within the Doors of disbanding. The band has taken on a curatorial role toward the old chaos monger, but the baby-sitting is getting to them. There seems to be a natural devolution in rock bands, a sort of expansion, which at some point demands dissolution, reconstruction, or (occasionally) human sacrifice. And Jim was already his own human sacrifice. Killed, shot, nightly on stage.

Doors' managers Sal Bonafede and Asher Dann are pressuring Morrison about going solo. The band members are spending more time with their girlfriends, Jim with his drinking buddies.

Once, he had been their kachina demon doll. "Jim was our puppet and we could take him with our music in any direction we wanted," John Densmore recalls. "When we started out we knocked them dead 90 percent of the time. Now we fucked up about 50 percent; 10 percent due to technical problems and 40 due to Jim."

But to Jim the failures were real; they were in some way as important to him as the triumphs. Success was, after all, part of the sickness, part of the platitudinous, cretinous American Dream, the Fat Dream. And hadn't all the Saints of Decadence declared with their very lives that failure was the badge of authenticity for the creator-madman?

&

On and on went the crusade. Jim—the Captain Ahab of rock—with his missionary zeal, railing, chiding audiences as if they were one giant being…Leviathan!

He could still be witty:

> Adolf Hitler is alive and well!
> [audience squirms and starts booing and hissing]
>
> I slept with her last night
> [audience cheers]
>
> You favor life, she favors death…and I'm on the fence and my balls hurt!
> [big cheers]

"**M**orrison hung there, very still, bathed in the red flood, with head dropped, eyes closed and arms outstretched—Christ on the cross. After the performance he gave, it was difficult to accept the cruci-fixion gesture without feeling that he was doing it to himself." (Photograph by Baron Wolman)

As John describes the last grueling tours of the Doors, you can feel the seething impatience and impotent rage. Jim telling interminable salty jokes to the audience, tumbling through songs, forgetting the words, stopping in the middle of songs…and he's not even drunk.

Rock evangelist Richard Sassin describes Jim Morrison-at-the-End in hallucinatory detail. The scene: Westbury Theater-in-the-Round on Long Island.

Morrison wasn't on stage when the music began. Suddenly there was a confrontation on one of the downhill aisles leading to the stage. He stumbled down the steps, entangling his black leather and a mass of tangled hair with the offstage darkness. He stopped to pose, and a flash of light caught him trying to regain his balance. The taunts began immediately. He responded with forced indifference or a threat of random violence.

The other Doors were in other rooms. They played on, almost oblivious to his ranting and raving. A familiar riff would begin, the audience would briefly come to attention, and he would leave the spotlight to inflict his boredom on them. He would fall into shadows searching for worthy opponents. There were glimpses of physical confrontations: crewcutted jocks protecting their interested girlfriends from his suggestions, Morrison's fist shooting blindly in the direction of obscene threats as a fat security guard grabs at him with a pathetic attempt to control the situation. Morrison embraces the guard and tries to pull him toward the stage while delivering a passionate plea for weight loss. The guard frees himself, runs up the aisle to derisive laughter, dropping his hat. Morrison tries to wear the hat but it is too small and suddenly he is disgusted with the whole scene and lets out a frenzied scream. Silence in the theater for the moment.

The audience stared as though it were another horrible car crash where the spirit was maimed and the blood ran into the gutter of the soul. Morrison twitched in some kind of death throes. The concert ended abruptly. Morrison howled but it was not with ecstasy. It was more Ginsberg than Blake. The lights came up before the band could walk back up the aisles and the audience booed. Morrison stood still

Jim: "The first time I saw the [concert] film I was rather taken aback.... I suddenly realized I was a puppet of a lot of forces I only vaguely understood." Old Minneapolis Auditorium, Minneapolis, Minn., 1969. (Photograph by Mike Barich)

listening. I stared so that my eyes would forever cover him. Some people were leaving, others still booing, a few watched him as intensely as I did. Then in this haphazard atmosphere he threw back his head and began to chant and dance in place like some possessed American Indian brave consecrating a sacred land, cleansing the abuse and disdain with singular belief so powerful that shivers ran through me. And my heart froze with undeniable blessing. A girl ran at him with scissors flashing to cut his hair and he disappeared into a circle of anonymous flesh that carried him away.

I loudly cursed the audience as we exited. We had to run and lock ourselves in the car to escape their retribution. They banged on the roof, threatening us. I told the driver to just take off, and soon we were on the Expressway speeding into the seventies.

Finally, there came a night when the flame began to futter. Playing at a place called the Warehouse (where do werewolves live?), Jim's spirit is fading. (During that set in New Orleans, Ray sees all of Jim's psychic energy go out the top of his head.) John sees it as the retribution of Jes Grew:

> There was an eerie mood that night. And it was coming from Jim. Someone must've been sticking pins in his psyche, because five years of bizarre vibes came to an abrupt halt. Rock had its origins here in N.O. Could it have been the voodoo revenge?

JOHN BARLEYCORN

Jim is spending more and more time in the Palms Bar with his mates.

Pantagruelian boozing, worthy of that "ever-thirsting" giant: "Drinks all 'round! Here, man, hold my coat!" Take my pants, too, while you're at it! Let's give 'em something to talk about!

Drinking, once taboo in hippie culture (Uncle Jack), had by the late sixties become common. Jimi Hendrix was doing more whiskey and reds than acid. Janis Joplin when she wasn't doing dope was consuming a couple of quarts of

Southern Comfort a day. That whole rap about alcohol, downers, protecting, sealing in the vision. The avatars were leaking. Cosmic dust spill.

A night of serious drinking. *I get drunk so I can talk to assholes. This includes me.* Oh Jim! At the bar in the stripper joint talking that talk. Growly, bemused, rowdy, world-weary, hip. Non sequitur city, baby! Rimbaud and Remy. His now charming, now threatening Southern drawl. Talking like the Duke & Dauphin in *Huck Finn.* Now he's the earnest ardent film school student, the *poète maudit*, the metaphysical wrangler (say what?). Mojo Man. And he's got a question for you:

> I fell asleep in the light of the full moon one night and when I woke up it was the face of my mother looking down at me. Now what do you think about that? What do think that means?

One minute he's Peer Gynt, the next he's Mr. Hyde, Admiral Morrison. *Being drunk is a good disguise.*

Why did no one have the presence of mind to record one of these rambling wet-quarters-and-soggy-dollar-bills conversations?

Sea chanties ("Land Ho!"), ballads, blooze and Dogpatch geography ("Runnin' Blues," Jim's tribute to Otis Redding) are creeping into the song repertoire. Comes from spending all that time down in Tangie Town.

> Miss Maggie M'Gill, she lived on a hill,
> Her daddy got drunk, and left her no will
> So she went down, down to "Tangie Town"
> People down there really like to get it on.
>
> "Maggie M'Gill"

The Clancy Brothers! It's the sort of stuff you can roar out over a Rams game with twelve simultaneous conversations going on and "Ode to Billie Jo" playing on the juke box.

Booze and blooze and Christmas trees.

At the very bottom of the Hindu caste system: actors, drunkards, snakes and rocks.

In the beginning it was amazing how many Jims he could juggle at the same time: teen idol, fashion plate, mystic, hippie, poet, lout. Here it's a little disconcerting how well he could tune in to that teen wavelength. (Photograph by Michael Ochs Archives/Venice, Calif.)

Within my bowl there lies
Shining dizziness,
Bubbling drunkenness.

There are great whirlwinds
Standing upside down above us.
They lie within my bowl.

A great bear heart,
A great eagle heart,
A great hawk heart,
A great twisting wind —
All those have gathered here
And lie within my bowl.

Now you will drink it.

Papago Indian "Song of Encouragement,"
translated by Ruth Underhill

And Jim seemed to know exactly what he was doing:

Getting drunk is…getting drunk. You're in complete control…up to a point, it's your choice, every time you take a
sip, you have a lot of small choices. It's like…I guess it's the
difference between suicide and slow capitulation.

Jim lad! The doomed, glass-clinking bard—and that was
his job, godammit, wasn't it?—fulfilling the poetic tradition
to which he'd apprenticed himself since greenest youth.

F. Scott Fitzgerald's line that there are no second acts in
American life. It's because Americans are romantics, the
spurting, exploding, imploding, self-detonating astounding-
ness, the suffering-as-an-attribute-of-god.

SHEDDING SKIN

Like the salamander he was, Jim's solution was to shed his
old skin and simply strike up a new identity.

Producer Paul Rothchild had told him, "Jim, you don't
look like a rock star anymore."

An oleaginous memo from the publicity department
("Jim Morrison, Renaissance Man") attempts, with some
spectacular hokum, to promote the image of Jim Morrison
at the expense of the Doors.

Jim rips it up. He loathes his public image; it's certainly not something he's going to aid and abet. He's been ripping down that cursed poster for years now, the one of that jerky guy posing with his shirt off.

> I think I was just fed up with the image that had been created around me, which I sometimes consciously, most of the time unconsciously, cooperated with. It was just too much for me to stomach and so I just put an end to it in one glorious evening.

Jim still doesn't get it. The show will go on, with or without him. And if he won't cooperate, if he won't shave off his beard, lose weight and (godammit!) at least *look* like himself, well, they'll just have to do it for him.

The record company, the publicity department…they all start behaving as if he's already gone. The current Morrison model (beard, overalls) simply does not exist. They start putting old photos of him on the live and best-of albums, *Absolutely Live* and *13*. Indeed, parts of the later albums are put together as if Jim were already dead, like the Jim Reeves TV offer. Poems, lyrics, fragments that Jim had done on various vocal takes are spliced together—like a dub record!

੨

Eventually, Jim came to see his perfection as a kind of inverse deformity. He was trying to erase it, that perfect face, that blandness, to smudge it like a face in a Francis Bacon portrait. A Neoplatonic face that Michelangelo had had to *invent* for his beautiful monster in the Piazza had been given to Morrison in the flesh on some sort of cosmic whim. Beauty as a gift; a "talent," as Janis would say. It's a sign. You are blessed. You are beautiful. People love you for that alone.

Jim's obsession with cripples, the sense that beauty, that kind of beauty, is a form of freakishness. Then he went—overnight!—from looking like Adonis to…Jerry Garcia! The quantum metamorphosis not only sudden, but utter. From adolescent god to Old Testament prophet in the twinkling of an eye.

Full beard, tinted aviator glasses, striped cotton railroad pants, smoking a cigar. The hair is no longer tousled, cheeks no longer gaunt. Jim has a paunch. The leather and beads are gone. He gets thrown out of clubs, maced by cops in his own dressing room. When Americans want to be taken seriously, they get fat and grow a beard. Orson Welles, Francis Ford Coppola. This was Jim's way of saying he'd changed. All that Pop star shit: the leather pants, the Russian peasant collars, the Navajo concho belt. Gone.

And the people who had kissed his ass didn't even recognize him. One of those movies where the other Jim is cryogenically stored somewhere. Two Jims! Two-Time Baby, Mr. Mojo. But whatever he imagined himself to be (and Jim could imagine almost anything) that Barbie Jim would still be there, it had a life of his own.

People around him are trying to see this change in the best light possible. Bill Siddons: "Jim used to have a lot of demons running about inside him. I don't think he has so many any more." Yeah, just one big bad one.

POETRY #3

Spring 1969. Private editions of Jim's books, *The Lords* and *The New Creatures*, are published. *The Lords* is a collection of aphorisms and aperçus on film, society, other topics. Stuff that had been percolating since his days at UCLA Film School. *The New Creatures* is a book of poems. A terrible bestiary, really, full of emblematic animals, ideas with legs, naked animism. A catalog of pain, death, assassination, evil snake root, people dancing on broken bones, riots, artists in hell, earthquakes and ghost children.

The last poem, the one that begins with the soft parade winding down Sunset, is an enthusiast's tour of the wasteland, a classic postapocalyptic theme for Jim. But the Wasteland has quite a different connotation for Jim than it had for T. S. Eliot. *This could be fun to rule a wasteland.*

The Lords & The New Creatures is later published by

Simon & Schuster. The back-cover blurb reads:

> Like Arthur Rimbaud before him, Morrison's life and vision led him to an exploration of the dark underbelly of his society. He emerged with images that seethe with the liquid heat of the city, the casual danger of the drug scene, and an unrestrained voyage into sensuality.

"Poetry is the language of the state of crisis," said Mallarmé, and Jim's poetry, with its jump cuts and strobe-light effects, is the log of an interior landscape in upheaval. (In *The New Creatures* these effects are a little stilted, possibly because of too much polishing and pedestal carving.)

The fragmentary nature of his posthumous collections, *Wilderness* and *The American Night,* is actually an asset. Indeed, fragments have done an immense amount for various people's reputations: Heraclitus, F. Scott Fitzgerald, Nietzsche, Taylor Mead.

In these rambling collections, his poetry has shaken loose from the studied word collisions of his first book. Canny, off-hand notations, clusters of dialogue and self-consciousness have given way to an unflinching self-scrutiny. *But I deserve this, great cannibal of all. Get on with the disease.*

Morrison was a Celt—*heir of the Mystery Christians, Snake in the Glen*—and the Celt, being by nature long-winded, when the wind gives out you know it's near the end. It is a rambling, wayward, crooked way. The mind-boggling *endlessness* of it. ("Digressions are sunshine," said Laurence Sterne, the most tangential of all writers.)

The Celtic eddy. The chaos that preceded order and underlies it. (*What* order?) Eddies, whorls and gnarls, the energy vortices, swirling around centers of source. Eruptions as phallic as Cu Chulainn's warp-spasm: "He blew up and swelled like a bladder full of breath and bent himself into a hideous arch, mottled and terrifying." And the way he sang, a keening chant, as if kodaking those lyrics: Kirillian phono-graphs.

FOLLOWING SPREAD

Martyr for an invisible crime, conjurer of syncretistic snakes with his attorney Max Fink at the Los Angeles Federal Building to appear before the U.S. Commissioner for extradition proceedings to Florida. He had been charged with lewd and lascivious behavior (among six other indictments) during a performance in Miami earlier in the year. April 14, 1969. (Photograph courtesy of UPI/Bettman)

THE END

An oppressive sense of impending doom. Like the actor who has played a role so long that he has become it, Jim is the Doomed Character. People around him begin having premonitions of Jim's death. Almost routinely, after every weekend there is some new rumor.

Paul Rothchild, after one of Jim's binges tells the group to get as much tape on Jim as fast as possible because he didn't think he was going to be around long.

December 8, 1969. Two polaroids of Jim on his twenty-sixth birthday from *No One Here Gets Out Alive:*

> "Oh, Christ, look!…Look at Jim!"…Slumped unconscious on his chair, Jim had managed to extract his penis from his pants and was pissing on the rug.

> Jim put the paper down. He shifted the bulk of his body and cleared his throat. "I think," he said slowly, "I'm having a nervous breakdown."

March 1970. Morrison Hotel reestablishes the Doors as a favorite with the critics. They are the first hard rock American band to achieve five gold albums consecutively.

Jim is singing with backup bands in North Beach topless clubs. There are over twenty paternity suits pending against him.

Midsummer Night 1970. Jim Morrison and Patricia Kennely, a writer for *Jazz & Pop* magazine, are married in a Wicca ceremony. Just like Henry VIII and Anne Boleyn are supposed to have done. The marriage certificate is written in runes. They sign it with their own blood. Jim faints.

August 15, 1970. Last public performance of the Doors, at the Isle of Wight Festival in England.

September 18, 1970. While in court in Miami, Morrison reads that Jimi Hendrix has died that morning in London. "Does anyone believe in omens?"

In the blur of trance a thousand demons dance within that fitful head. Old Minneapolis Auditorium, 1969. (Photograph by Mike Barich)

FOLKTALE

His life a variation on the Changeling fable. A folktale bargain: The price of fame, genius, immortality is death. At the crossroads where Robert Johnson sold his soul to the devil to play the blues, where ghosts interest travelers in their fate, the Hitchhiker takes a drink of whiskey and calls *again on the dark hidden gods of the blood*. They answer: *Why do you call us? You know our price. It never changes.*

Like all who make a pact with the devil, Jim believed there must be an escape clause. But whatever he did he would always be Jim Morrison, Pop Star, playing at being a poet. Any extracurricular activity undertaken by a star would be a pretense, like Marie Antoinette tending sheep.

The story of someone who led a charmed life, even if it turned out ultimately to be treacherous. The ferocity with which he had believed in things and made them come true. A whole lifetime spent believing in fanciful ideas begotten by desire upon impossibility. Everything he'd done since adolescence had been based on some outrageous premise or other—dead poets, epileptic painters, phantoms and witch doctors....In the light of this, his new incarnation as the retiring poet of Axel's Castle was not quite as absurd as it seemed. "I'm not denying that I've had a good time these past three or four years," he told Salli Stevenson, an interviewer for *Circus* magazine, during the Miami trial. "I've met a lot of interesting people and seen things in a short space of time that I probably wouldn't have run into in twenty years of living. I can't say I regret it. But if I had to do it over...I think I would have gone for the quiet, undemonstrative artist-plodding-away-in-his-own-garden trip."

ENVOI

Spring 1971. The Doors are recording their last album. *L.A. Woman* c'est moi. The way Jim howls down those words. The angelo he puts on every syllable. Mexican nights, neon, existential dread, the end of time, the wind howling at the edge of the world.

That image of Jim in *No One Here Gets Out Alive:*

> The solitary, overweight figure in the rumpled fatigue jacket
> and jeans, with massive head and face of hair, moved slowly
> along the Hollywood streets. Day after day Jim walked,
> looking at the stucco wonderland as if for the final time.

A weary curator of the city he and the Doors had
unearthed, not in the way New Yorkers and other sasse-
nachs are perpetually "discovering" L.A. (men watering the
lawn in their pajamas). Jim was of it; L.A. was his
Herculaneum, his Angkor Wat. What they had excavated
was a proleptic city of anxious pleasures *preyed upon by savage
bands of youths.* An archeology of the future where the ruins
are so perfectly preserved from the climate that historians
decide to rent out the strange dwellings until some sense
can be made of them.

He packed up his books, his journals, his life. Perhaps he
intended to meditate on L.A. from exile. And in his Paris
journal (in *The American Night*) he did so with remorseful
fury. He thought about doing a show with Fred Myrow on
the subject.

> What we wanted to crystallize or capture was the moment
> of transition when we all felt so strongly in Los Angeles in
> the late sixties and early seventies. What'd Huxley say:
> "Between the evergreens something was lurking."

At the same time, the toxicity of the city was getting to
him. *Off-on, on and off, like one long sick electric dream.* He was
talking to his publisher about doing an impressionistic auto-
biography, some fragments of which seem to be in the "As I
Look Back" section of *Wilderness.*

Another (darker) self-portrait of sorts can be found in his
"Ode to L.A. While Thinking of Brian Jones, Deceased,"
full of Hockney paper pools (all the splashes are in italics)
with real horrors skulking around the edges. As he contem-
plates Brian, *in meat heaven w/cannibals and jews,* he hopes the
dark star of the Rolling Stones went out with a smile on his
face *into the cool remnants of a dream.*

If this reflective mood in his last days in L.A. suggests a mellower, more restrained Jim, that impression would be mistaken. He is still out there, pickled and dusted, ten stories above the Strip, walking along narrow railings.

His last day, for example. "It was pure hell," recalls Patricia Kennely. "It started at four at some topless-bottomless coed bar where we had so many tequilas with beer chasers that the bartender was sending every third drink over free. Last I remember I'd had fourteen."

The next day Jim leaves for Paris.

PARIS

Summer 1971. There is a certain predictability to these days in Paris, Jim's last. A sense of fading out. The last days of Oscar Wilde. The man whose life had been purloined and who was going to begin all over again. A phantom that you can already see through. In this state death is a mere formality. *Quand tu veux, monsieur, quand tu veux.*

Like Kerouac's account of his breakdown (in *Big Sur*), the world just didn't mean that much to Jim anymore. The people he ran into—old friends or people he'd just met—came away with the sense that they had met an impostor. He spoke of the weather, the rate of exchange. He seemed drained, like Poe's "The Man Who Was Used Up." "I'm so sick of everything…I'd be so glad if people didn't recognize me…who do they think Jim Morrison is, anyway?"

He was also Ubu Roi, Alfred Jarry's Dada king, shouting obscenities, mumbling to himself, declaiming verse to astonished pedestrians on the Pont Neuf, violently berating French businessmen lunching at expensive bistros, calling doormen and bouncers niggers, falling down, throwing up, sleeping it off on park benches, arriving at the apartments of strangers and moving in.

And then, on July 3, 1971, he ran himself a hot bath. "I figured you took a big snort, had some Courvoisier, climbed into the tub…and goodnight," John Densmore speculates.

When the still sea conspires an armor
And her sullen and aborted
Currents breed tiny monsters,
True sailing is dead.

Awkward instant
And the first animal is jettisoned,
Legs furiously pumping
Their stiff green gallop,
And heads bob up
Poise
Delicate
Pause
Consent
In mute nostril agony
Carefully refined and sealed over

"Horse Latitudes"

After he had been in the bathroom a very long time, and Pamela could not open the door, she telephoned one of her lovers, Jean DeBetti, and then called Marianne Faithfull: "Jim is in the bathroom. The door is locked. I can't get him out. Will you come over immediately?"

When Faithfull and DeBetti arrive, they help Pamela pry open the door. Inside, they find Jim is dead in the bathtub. Wondering what to do next, Pamela and DeBetti do some dope. DeBetti, a French count, is himself dead within a year of a heroin OD. Pamela ODs two years after that. To friends, she says that she feels responsible for Jim's death because it was her stash that killed him.

DeBetti calls in a French doctor to sign the death certificate. Since it is a national holiday in France, Jim cannot be buried for at least three days. They lift him out of the bath, put him on the dining room table, pack him in ice cubes and wrap him in plastic.

On Tuesday, a coffin is finally procured. This is the day Bill Siddons, the group's manager, arrives. John recalls Siddons' account of what he found:

The casket was right there in the bedroom so you can imagine the vibes in the place. I never thought to see the body, as Pam was obviously shattered. [Hence, the beginning of fake death rumors.] Once, while alone in the living room, I opened a carved box on the coffee table and found white powder in a clear envelope. Pam was in the kitchen, so I decided to try a little to see what it was. It wasn't coke. Soon afterward I became nauseous and felt very sick. It sure was something I never tried before.

So there he sleeps, in the Père Lachaise Cemetery in Paris, in the shadow of the massive Beaux Arts markers. In the company of Oscar Wilde, Chopin, Edith Piaf and Balzac, his grave scrawled like a palimpsest with messages from fans.

CANCEL MY SUBSCRIPTION TO THE RESURRECTION

Morrison was a film school student possessed. He saw his life at 24 frames per second with the Doors' music as its soundtrack, and would have found it entirely fitting that his most recent incarnation should be as a movie star (in Oliver Stone's *The Doors*). Indeed, a previous resurrection (circa 1980) had also come about because of a movie.

The use of the Doors' eerily crooned "The End" on the soundtrack of *Apocalypse Now* was so right, so timely, it seemed as if it had been written for the film.

Martin Sheen's left eye drifts through Southeast Asian jungles like a detached retina from *Le Chien Andalou*, swimming past exotic palm trees, sampans sailing on ancient rivers, pyrotechnic displays—paradise in flames! The disconcerting mix of exotica and horror is the perfect visual counterpoint to the Doors song. A bamboo jazz dribbling guitar, the ironic carnival organ, the court-martial percussion—all uncannily driving the torch song as it phantasmagorically turns to dust. The music so in sync with the images that it might have been encephalographically transmitted from the sleeping brain of Jim Morrison, dead in the Père Lachaise Cemetery these twenty years.

Acknowledgments

My first debt is to those who blazed the trail in the Saga Morrisoniana, Jerry Hopkins and Danny Sugerman's *No One Here Gets Out Alive* and John Densmore's *Riders on the Storm*. Without these two books I would have been lost in the wilderness. I am additionally grateful to Danny Sugerman for his assistance in enabling me to obtain permission to quote the Doors' lyrics.

I have also drawn on materials from the *Phoenix Gazette*, Kris Weintraub in *Crawdaddy*, Jerry Hopkins' interview with Jim Morrison in *Rolling Stone*, Richard Goldstein in the *Village Voice*, Jon Mendelsohn in the *Los Angeles Times*, Phil Kirby in the *Daily Brain*, Salli Stevenson in *Circus* magazine and Isaac Asimov's *Foundation and Empire*.

My thanks to Richard Sassin for writing his *cinema apocalyptique* account of Morrison at the Westbury Theater-in-the-Round for this book; Lenny Kaye for letting me cannibalize some of his best lines from our joint venture, *Rock 100;* Mark Johnson for his ears; and Nick Tosches for the Foreword.

To my editor, Jim Fitzgerald, for his encouragement and enthusiasm, and to the ever-forbearing Alex Kuczynski.

Special thanks to Tony Secunda for getting me involved in this project, and to Carol Mann for working it out (and Christine Lazor for perennial good spirits).

The envelope please…Kathleen and Linda Gates for production under fire, Louise Marinis for line editing, Peter C. Jones for diplomacy, Catherine Schurdak for sweet reasonableness, and that old curmudgeon, J.-C. Suarès, for his elegant design.

And, last but not least, Coco for the alchemy of the word.

FACING PAGE

Jim, c'mon, man, don't do that spooky stuff. Mojo lays the Old Man of the Mountains Zugs-iz-Zees wink on yer. Garden District Restaurant, Los Angeles, Calif., 1970. (Photograph by Andrew Kent)

This is the London Fog, the virtual Sea of Galilee of Doors mythology where the Fisher King first dipped his gnostic nets. Or, rather, this *was* the London Fog, now the Central. But, wait, in this picture it is the Fog again. Nevermind, it's the Sunset Strip location from Oliver Stone's *The Doors*. (Photograph by Heather Harris)

DESIGN: J.-C. Suarès/Spade & Archer, Inc.
PICTURE EDITOR: Peter C. Jones
MANAGING EDITOR: Catherine Schurdak
PICTURE COORDINATOR: Lisa S. Adelson
COPY EDITOR: Louise Marinis
PRODUCTION: Gates Studio

Doors reflected in windows. Sausalito docks, outside of San Francisco, Calif., 1967. (Photograph © 1967 Bobby Klein, courtesy FAHEY/KLEIN Gallery, Los Angeles)